Bloody Banners
and
Barefoot Boys

Unidentified Northern Alabama Soldier

BLOODY BANNERS

AND

BAREFOOT BOYS

"A HISTORY OF THE
27TH REGIMENT ALABAMA INFANTRY CSA"
The Civil War Memoirs and Diary Entries of J. P. Cannon M.D.

Compiled and Edited
by
Noel Crowson
and
John V. Brogden

 Burd Street Press

This Burd Street Press book
was printed by
Beidel Printing House, Inc.
63 West Burd Street
Shippensburg, PA 17257 USA

In respect for the scholarship contained herein, the acid-free paper used in this book meets the guidelines for permanence and durability of the Committee on Production Guidelines for Book Longevity of the Council on Library Resources.

For a complete list of available publications
please write
Burd Street Press
Division of White Mane Publishing Company, Inc.
P. O. Box 152
Shippensburg, PA 17257 USA

Library of Congress Cataloging-in-Publication Data

Cannon, J. P., b. 1843.
    Bloody banners and barefoot boys : a history of the 27th Regiment
Alabama Infantry CSA : the Civil War memoirs and diary entries of
J. P. Cannon, M.D. / compiled and edited by Noel Crowson and John
V. Brogden.
        p.   cm.
    Includes bibliographical references and index.
    ISBN 1-57249-018-7 (alk. paper)
    1. Confederate States of America.   Army.   Alabama Infantry
Regiment, 27th.   2.   United States--History--Civil War, 1861–1865-
-Regimental histories.   3.   Alabama--History--Civil War, 1861–1865-
-Regimental histories.   4.   United States--History--Civil War,
1861–1865--Personal narratives, Confederate.   5.   Alabama--History-
-Civil War, 1861–1865--Personal narratives.   6.   Cannon, J. P., b.
1843--Diaries.   7.   Soldiers--Alabama--Lauderdale County--Diaries.
8.   Lauderdale County (Ala.)--Biography.   I.   Crowson, Noel, 1947–
.   II.   Brogden, John V., 1950–   .   III.   Title.
E551.5 27th.C36   1997
973.7'461--dc21   96-40234
                                                                        CIP

Table of Contents

Acknowledgments

The editors of this work wish to acknowledge that this book would not have been possible without the efforts of Dr. J. P. Cannon. It was during research on the military record of Capt. H. B. Irwin (great-uncle of the wife of one of the editors) and of the records of the Crowson brothers who served in Co. I, that Dr. Cannon's work was located at the Alabama State Archives. The manuscript had been serialized under the title *Inside of Rebeldom* in 1910 in issues of the *Washington National Tribune*, but was otherwise unpublished. Other works which must be credited are Barnard's book, *Tattered Volunteers, The 27th Alabama Infantry Regiment*, an excellent historical and geographical supplement to the personal observations of Dr. Cannon. Dr. Cannon served as a private in the ranks of the 27th. When these two works are combined by the reader, no finer or more detailed history of a Civil War Regiment can be found.

Thanks should also go to Michael Winey of the National Military History Institute at Carlisle Barracks, Pennsylvania. His assistance in the location and acquisition of photographs of men in the 27th was invaluable. The staff at the Wheeler Basin Regional Library in Decatur, Alabama; the Lawrence County Historical Commission in Moulton, Alabama; and the Civil War historian Robert Parham of Decatur, Alabama were equally helpful with their assistance and direction. We would also not want to forget the National Archives in Washington, D.C., who were responsible for much of the research and compilation of individual service records.

Because of the preponderance of material provided by Dr. Cannon's manuscript, the following pages are our tribute and small token of appreciation for his life and effort. The obituaries for Dr. Cannon and his wife appeared in the *Confederate Veteran Magazine*, a publication supported by Dr. Cannon from its inception until his death.

vii

Tribute to Dr. J. P. Cannon

The following obituaries appeared in *the Confederate Veteran Magazine*, for both Dr. J. P. Cannon and his wife. Rather than attempt to write some introduction for Dr. Cannon, these editors felt that no finer description of this man, his family, and his life than the reprints of these articles could be given.

Mrs. J. P. Cannon.

Mrs. J. P. Cannon died at her home, in McKenzie, Tenn., on the evening of February 4, in her sixty-fifth year. Mrs. Cannon's illness dated back for a period of three years; but for the past few months she had been declining rapidly, and her death was not unexpected.

On the afternoon that her friends gathered to pay a last tribute to her memory the house would not hold the throng of those who had come to mourn for her. She had lived a full and beautiful Christian life, and among the wide circle of those who loved her she will be missed in every place where womanly goodness and gentleness are the things that count.

She is survived by her husband (Dr. J. P. Cannon), three daughters (Mesdames R. B. Moore, of McKenzie, A. J. Smith, of Clinton, Ky., and Horace Jordan, of Camden), two sons (Lloyd and Turner Cannon, of McKenzie), a brother (W. L. Carroll), and a sister (Mrs. W. B. Everett).

Dr. J. P. Cannon.

Many beautiful and loving tributes have been paid to the life of Dr. J. P. Cannon, of McKenzie, Tenn.; but to me it seems that the real place for a sketch of his life is in the beloved *Veteran*. He was devoted to its pages, having been a lifelong subscriber, and treasured every copy. He was an active leader in the Stonewall Jackson Bivouac of this place, a member of the Board of Directors of the Confederate Home, and gave many days in helping to obtain comforts for the old soldiers, widows' pensions, etc., and his name is enshrined in the hearts of Veterans, Sons, and Daughters of the Confederacy.

Dr. Cannon was a man of positive character, positive faith, positive opinions, positive actions, yet as gentle and unobtrusive as it is possible for one to be. Sweet modesty, calmness, and genuine goodness could not reside in a breast that was not enriched with the noblest virtues and grandeur of soul. His book, "Inside of Rebeldom," the daily life of this splendid soldier, reveals the bright mind of a thorough Southern gentleman.

He was born at Gravelly Springs, Ala., April 19, 1843. He enlisted in Company C, 27th Alabama Regiment, in December, 1861, and was paroled in May, 1865. He was married to Miss Kate Walker Carroll, who died a few years ago. Five children survive him: Mesdames May Moore, Madge Smith, Maude Jordon, and Lloyd and Turner Cannon.

[Mrs. E. K. Higgins.]

Introduction

When I first consented to write the history of the 27th Alabama, it was with a feeling of my incompetency to do justice to a regiment which made so honorable a record during the trying times of 1861–1865. As no one else seemed inclined or willing to undertake the work, it has fallen upon me, and I will endeavor to write a plain, unvarnished narrative of its service.

Being engaged in a business which requires all my attention, I will be unable to give the subject the thought and research it deserves, but will quote liberally from a diary kept during the war, which has been published under the title *Inside of Rebeldom*. A few items have been gleaned from *Perry and Smith's Montgomery Directory* and *Brewer's Alabama*. These and my own memory comprise the only sources of my information, with the exception of the very few facts obtained from surviving comrades.

The 27th Alabama was mustered into the service of the Confederate States at Florence, Alabama on December 24th, 1861. The field officers had been previously elected as follows:

A. A. Hughes, Colonel   James Jackson, Lt. Colonel
Dr. Edward McAlexander, Major

Colonel Hughes was a member of the Alabama Legislature at the beginning of the war, but resigned and returned to Franklin County to assist in raising the regiment and was then elected Colonel. Hughes was captured at Fort Donelson in February 1862, exchanged in September 1862 and died the following October of that same year.

Lieutenant Colonel Jackson, of Lauderdale County, enlisted as a private in the 4th Alabama in the spring of 1861. Jackson was severely wounded at First

Manassas, discharged and after recovering assisted in raising the 27th Alabama. He was elected Lt. Colonel, and after the death of Col. Hughes, was promoted to Colonel of the regiment. In June of 1864, he was wounded in the arm which necessitated amputation. He recovered and was again in command of the remnant of the brigade when the army surrendered at Greensboro, North Carolina on April 26, 1865.

Dr. McAlexander was practicing his profession in Lauderdale County, and in the fall of 1861 took an active part in organizing the regiment. He was elected 1st Lieutenant of Company C, promoted to Major and later to Lt. Colonel. McAlexander was in command of the consolidated regiment at the close of the war.

It was my desire to give the names and short sketches of all the company officers, but survivors having failed to respond to my earnest requests for information, I find it impracticable to make a complete roster. Therefore, to avoid the appearance of partiality, I deem it best to omit special mention and name only the first company commanders and the counties from which they enlisted.

Company A	Capt. J. E. Moore	Franklin County
Company B	Capt. R. G. Wright	Franklin County
Company C	Capt. E. B. Thompson	Lauderdale County
Company D	Capt. H. B. Irwin	Lawrence County
Company E	Capt. T. A. Jones	Lauderdale County
Company F	Capt. M. P. Roberts	Madison County
Company G	Capt. T. E. McCulloch	Franklin County
Company H	Capt. Humphrey	Morgan County
Company I	Capt. Dr. H. L. Ray	Lauderdale County
Company K	Capt. H. A. McGenee	Lawrence County

JPC

Organization of the Regiment

Bloody Banners and Barefoot Boys

In the fall of 1861, it was generally believed and so published in the newspapers, that the Federals were planning an invasion by way of the Tennessee and Cumberland Rivers, and this news created a sensation throughout North Alabama. The war was coming to our very doors: our negroes would be freed, stock driven off, and the beautiful valley of the Tennessee devastated. The time had come for every man to "shoulder his gun". President Davis issued an urgent call for volunteers, stating in the call that the men must arm themselves, as he had no arms to give them.

There were no examinations by surgeons as to physical condition, nor were youth or old age a bar to eligibility: every man or boy capable of handling a gun was gladly received and no questions were asked. We were entertained with red hot speeches, picturing in glowing terms the glorious destiny of the "young nation which had just been born", and urged to hurry or the boys in Virginia would clean out the Yankees before we had a chance to show our mettle.

The roll of the drum and shrill note of the fife could be heard all over the land, while the work of collecting arms and other necessaries progressed. Double barrelled shot guns were the only weapons available, which the majority of us already possessed, and those who had not were soon accommodated by neighbors who were willing to contribute that much to the cause. Bayonets would have been useless appendages with our shot guns, but it looked more "warlike" to have something of the kind, and it was decided that long "Bowie knives" would be the best substitute and the most easily obtained: accordingly a search was begun for material from which to manufacture them. Almost every farm had a blacksmith shop in

1

those days, and in them were large files and rasps which had been worn out and laid aside as useless. These and any other pieces of steel which could be made into knives were hunted up and the ring of the blacksmith's hammer could be heard in every shop. The blacksmiths fashioned these once peaceful instruments into weapons which were to exterminate all the Yankees who should have the temerity to come up the Tennessee River.

Organization of the Regiment

By the 24th of December 1861, ten companies of about 100 each had been enrolled and assembled in Florence where we elected Field Officers as follows: A. A. Hughes of Franklin County, Colonel James Jackson of Lauderdale County, Lieutenant Colonel Dr. Richard McAlexander of Lauderdale County, Major. The companies were organized as follows:

Company A	Capt. J. E. Moore	Franklin County
Company B	Capt. R. G. Wright	Franklin County
Company C	Capt. E. B. Thompson	Lauderdale County
Company D	Capt. H. B. Irwin	Lawrence County
Company E	Capt. T. A. Jones	Lauderdale County
Company F	Capt. M. P. Roberts	Madison County
Company G	Capt. T. E. McCulloch	Franklin County
Company H	Capt. Humphrey	Morgan County
Company I	Capt. Dr. H. L. Ray	Lauderdale County
Company K	Capt. H. A. McGenee	Lawrence County

We were mustered into the service of the Confederate States by General S. D. Weakly of Florence. In the afternoon of the same day, with our 1000 double barrelled shot guns and our 1000 long Bowie Knives, we proudly marched to the river where a boat was waiting to bear us "to the war".

Like all fresh regiments, we had baggage enough to have supplied a brigade twelve months later. In short, we were fully equipped for house keeping with the single exception that we had no feather beds, the nearest approach to that article of luxury being the ticks which we carried for the purpose of filling with straw after we reached our destination. After a last farewell to the anxious friends who had followed us thus far, we loosened the lines and amidst cheers and the waving of handkerchiefs we steamed out down the "Blue Tennessee".

The trip was uneventful, and on the morning of December 26th, we arrived at Fort Henry, a small fort on the east bank of the river in Stewart County, Tennessee. It had 10 or 15 guns, chiefly small ones, but it looked formidable to us, who had never seen anything like it before. We were not allowed to land, but proceeded to the opposite side of the river in Calloway County, Kentucky. Here it was intended for us to build a fort, which with the assistance of Fort Henry, was to create an impassable barrier to all craft and sink the Lincoln Gunboats to the bottom of the river, if they should have the audacity to attempt a passage.

Prepared for Winter

It required several days to complete our arrangements, such as laying off camps, stretching tents, building bunks, etc. but when it was all done, we were comfortably fixed for the winter and in our ignorance of a soldier's life and its uncertainties, felt like we had "come to stay."

Engineers planned our fort which we named "Heiman" in honor of the Colonel of the 10th Tennessee who commanded the forces on both sides of the river. Little work was done in the building of the fort and we spent the month of January in regular routine duties, many incidents occurring which seemed ludicrous after we became more seasoned soldiers. Our rations consisted of a fair article of beef and cornmeal, which was supplemented by luxuries we got from home on the steamboats which made regular trips, enabling us to fare sumptuously and we began to think a soldier's life not so bad as represented. Towards the latter part of the month, however, rumors of the advance of the enemy were circulated in camp and frequently we were roused from our slumbers by the "long roll" in the dead hours of the night. At first these false alarms caused a great deal of excitement and we tumbled out of our warm beds and began a search for clothing and accoutrements, which in our fancied security we had left scattered in disorder over the tents. It would have been amusing to an old soldier to have witnessed these scenes, but as all of us were "fresh" there was no one to criticise, and we soon "caught on" and came to the conclusion that night alarms were only a part of our regular drill and a nuisance besides.

Along in the first days of February, we could discern ominous clouds of black smoke rising from the river below, the source of which was hidden from view by a bend in the river, but evidently it proceeded from gunboats and reports came that the enemy was landing thousands of troops on the Fort Henry side and still Fort Heiman was only a fort in name. We had scarcely broken dirt and not a cannon was on our side of the river.*

* At that time, the 27th Alabama was brigaded with the 10th Tennessee, the 48th Tennessee, Captain Culbertson's battery of four pieces, and a Tennessee battalion of cavalry. The brigade was commanded by Colonel Heiman of the 10th Tennessee Regiment. Serial 7, page 137, Report of General Tilghman. Ed.

Battle of Fort Henry

About midnight, February 5th, we had another night alarm, this time not by the beating of the "long roll" but by soft tones from the officers who opened the flaps of tents and commanded, "Boys, get up quick, leave everything except guns and cartridge boxes. Fall in without a bit of noise." We had profited by previous training and had everything at hand, so it required but a short time to form line and march to the river, little dreaming that we were leaving our comfortable quarters, never to see them again.

Boarding the boat which was waiting for us, with lights all covered and with renewed caution to keep perfect silence, we steered direct to Fort Henry. The gunboats could not be seen on account of the darkness and consequently had no breakfast and no prospect of dinner. The morning hours passed slowly with couriers constantly passing in and out, but we could get no information from them.

Although we did hear that the country below us was just "swarming" with Yankees, we felt that the time was at hand when we would have an opportunity of testing our double-barrelled guns and bowie knives. An inspection showed that we had left our knives on the other side of the river; not half a dozen could be found in the regiment. Some were left sticking in trees where we had practised throwing them, others on stumps where the last beef had been carved, but the large part probably scattered about camps and tents.

We had literally obeyed orders, anyhow, for the officers had ordered us to leave everything except guns and cartridge boxes. Now we would have to depend on "buck and ball". Our ammunition consisted of paper cartridges carrying three buckshot and a round ball weighing about an ounce—similar to those used with the old fashioned musket.

We waited expectantly for something to "turn up", but no demonstration was made by land or water until a little after noon. We were startled by the discharge of heavy guns and big shells came crunching and crashing through the timber above our heads. It was a thrilling sensation to be under fire for the first time, every moment expecting the land forces to swoop down on us in overwhelming numbers. We had been led by couriers and cavalrymen to believe that there were ten to one, at least. We were vividly reminded of what the valiant orators, who were doing the wind work for the Confederacy, and urging the boys to go to the front at once and not miss the "glorious opportunity of expelling the ruthless invaders from our sacred southern soil", told us, i.e., that one southerner could whip five Yankees, ten to one was more than we had bargained for and when we were ordered to pile overcoats, load and cap our guns, it was with suppressed excitement that we awaited the approach of the enemy.

Our little fort replied as vigorously as it was capable; the booming of its guns mingled with those of the gunboats, the crashing of shells through the timber and falling of limbs around us seemed terrific to our unaccustomed ears. Though the real danger was small, as very few of the shells burst near our line, and being on lower ground than the fort, those which missed it went clean over our heads. The cannonading continued incessantly for about an hour and a half when it ceased as suddenly as it began.

Retreat to Fort Donelson

We were immediately ordered to "right face, forward march" up the river, which appeared a little strange as the enemy was supposed to be in the opposite direction, and for a short while we could not comprehend what had happened. It soon dawned upon us that the fort had surrendered and we were retreating, running from the Yankees. We, who had so recently left home with visions of glory to be achieved on the field of battle, of hundreds of Yankees to be slain with our "buck and ball" and our long-bladed knives steeped in Yankee gore, were actually running before we had fired a gun or even caught a glimpse of a blue-coat.

When it became known that we were retreating the impulse to go faster seemed to strike all of us at the same time, while the dashing past of small squads of frightened cavalrymen and an occasional shot in the rear served to accelerate our speed until it taxed to the utmost the capacity of short-legged fellows to keep up with the procession. We followed a dim road leading up the river and had not covered more than a mile when we were confronted by a perfect torrent of a creek which, swollen by recent rains, was rushing down from the hills toward the river like a mill race and was fully fifty feet wide.

Some of us (this writer among the number) had just broken out with the measles that morning and here was a predicament—a stream of cold water ahead, Yankees behind—either was bad enough, but time was too precious for dallying and of the two evils it required but a moment to choose the lesser of them. The stream was so deep and the current so strong that small men could not stem it alone, so locking together, tall and short, by fours we plunged in and all made a successful landing on the opposite shore. Following the course of the river several miles we turned across the country towards Fort Donelson, the enemy's cavalry charging upon our rear occasionally during the afternoon, but in small force and they were easily repulsed. Night ended the pursuit, but not our troubles for it set in cloudy and so dark we could not see our file leaders. All night long we groped our way over hills and hollows wading numberless creeks and branches and finally reached Fort Donelson at daylight, exhausted and almost starved. Truly we were in a sad plight: 36 hours without food and a 15 mile run through mud and water without a minute's rest was pretty rough on a lot of raw soldiers who had never seen any active service.

We got a good deal of experience crowded into a short space of time, but not much glory. Six weeks after we landed, our fort demolished, the Tennessee, which we went out to defend, opened to the head of navigation and was driven away with everything lost. There was not even an overcoat or blanket to protect us from the wintry winds, the snows and rains which prevailed at that season of the year.

Having no hospital accommodations at Fort Donelson, and very few tents, even the well men were much exposed to the inclement weather and as the sick would be only an incumbrance during the impending battle, they were hurried off as fast as the boats could carry them. Being one of those who was sent off to the hospital, I am unable to give details of the part the 27th Alabama played in the series of engagements which followed. I was informed, by members of the regiment who participated, that while under fire the greater part of the time the fighting on their part of the line was not as fierce as on their right, and consequently, losses were comparatively light.

Battle of Fort Donelson

On the 12th of February, skirmishing began between Forrest's cavalry and the advance of the enemy. The fighting was renewed early on the morning of the 13th, our cavalry driven in, and the battle was on in earnest. For three days it raged, attack after attack was made on our lines, our forces being uniformly successful in repelling the assaults of superior numbers. On the morning of the 15th, our forces assumed the offensive and a determined onslaught was made on the enemy's right wing, supposedly for the purpose of opening the way for a retreat. This was entirely successful, but from some cause or other, instead of withdrawing the army they were marched back to the breastworks and during the night it was decided to surrender. Our boys were very much surprised when they awoke on that memorable Sunday to see the white flag. Our generals have been severely criticised, but it does not come within the scope of this work to discuss that point; however, it is certain that quite a number did escape. Among the number were Captain R. G. Wright of Company B and Sergeant J. H. Chandler of Company C (afterwards 1st Lieutenant). Lieutenant Chandler says the officers were taken to Johnson's Island and the privates to Camp Douglas where they remained until exchanged in September 1862. I have recently written to some of the comrades to give me some of the details of their prison life, but in not a single instance have I obtained the desired information. Therefore, the history, so far as this point in time is concerned, must necessarily be a blank. No doubt it was similar to that of other prisoners of war, many of them died from sickness and exposure and have slept these forty odd years in northern soil, many familiar faces were absent when we were reunited the following December.

7

Off for Home

We will now follow the remnant of the regiment which escaped by reason of being in hospital, off on detail, and other causes. Having no command to go to, it was "every man for himself" and we made our way as best we could to our homes in North Alabama, where we found people in a turmoil of excitement. The disaster had a depressing effect on all, every vestige of defense upon which they relied had been swept away. All our armies retreated south of the Tennessee River and they felt that they were at the mercy of the enemy. Newspapers contained exaggerated accounts of depredations committed in Tennessee, which increased the panic among the citizens who were making hurried preparations to run off their negroes and bury their gold and other valuables.

We were in no great hurry to get back to the army and remained at our homes some two weeks, when we learned that Captains Roberts and Wright of the 27th were collecting the remnant of the regiment and, reporting promptly, we found about fifty of the boys in camps in Tuscumbia, Alabama. This number was recruited during the month of March to about one hundred and fifty, all that were left of the one thousand who had started out three months before. We organized into two companies and were taken under command, according to their respective ranks in the regiment, by an almost full complement of officers.

In the meantime, General Johnston had concentrated all available forces in the vicinity of Corinth, and General Grant was landing large numbers of troops at Pittsburgh Landing, which indicated that a battle of greater magnitude than any that had been fought in this Department was imminent. Consequently, we were not surprised when the roar of artillery was borne to us over the placid bosom of the Tennessee on that Sunday morning of April 6th. General Johnston was one of our ideal commanders and we had full confidence in his ability, with the vast army which he had collected, to retrieve the waning fortunes of the Confederacy.

Presuming that our little squad, so far from the scene of action, would be overlooked and being eager to "hear the drums of battle", we immediately telegraphed the General that we had 150 men at Tuscumbia subject to his orders, but no orders came then. We spent the whole of that bloody Sunday listening with intense anxiety to the storm raging around Shiloh Church.

Getting There Too Late

Early on Monday morning we received a reply to our telegram instructing us to come at once, and having neither baggage nor accoutrements, it required but a short time to roll up our blankets and hasten to the depot. The battle resumed and the rumble of guns, like distant thunder, was more constant, if possible, than on the preceding day. The most encouraging telegrams were constantly being received—our boys had driven a portion of the enemy into the river, captured many thousands of prisoners and were finishing the work begun on Sunday. This was the substance of the news which was passing over the wires, and while waiting impatiently for a train the telegraph office was the centre of attraction to get the latest.

It was the middle of the afternoon before our train arrived, which we boarded hoping to reach the scene of the conflict in time for the third day's battle, provided there was anything left for us to fight. We heard no more from the front during the short trip and when we reached Corinth we were stunned by the changed state of affairs; the battle had closed, the victory of Sunday had been turned into defeat on Monday and our army was in retreat.

The town was full of stragglers, hundreds of wounded were being brought in and when we saw the suffering and heard the groans of the unfortunates we felt some satisfaction that we had not arrived in time to participate in the battle. We were thankful that we were alive and sound in body, which would not have been the case with some of us, but for the delays under which we had been chafing the last two days. Depressed in spirits and mourning the loss of their commander, the army continued its retreat and within a few days settled down in camps around the town.

Our two little companies were in a pitiable condition. Without arms, without a command which we could call our own, we felt lonesome in the midst of an army of 50,000. Like orphans we were buffeted about from place to place receiving orders one day which were countermanded the next. We finally landed in the 51st Tennessee with which we had the promise of a permanent location until our own regiment should be exchanged. We had hardly been with the 51st long enough to learn the names of the officers, when we were ordered to report to General Ruggles for artillery service.

We immediately called a meeting of the two companies and it was unanimously voted that we did not want any artillery service "in ours". We had volunteered as infantry and proposed to stick to that arm of the service, but how to avoid it was the question which agitated our minds.

We sent up a petition, requesting a countermand of the order, but knew it could not go through the regular channel and return by the time we were to report to General Ruggles. So, some suggested that all report sick thus staving it off one day longer, which would give us a little more time to consider the matter.

A Successful Ruse

When the drum beat sick call, 150 of us fell into line and marched up to the surgeon's tent. What he thought of such a procession he did not divulge, but began examining at the head of the column. One had a backache, another rheumatism, another a bad stomachache, and so forth on through the list of diseases as far as our limited vocabulary of names could be remembered.

He had examined a dozen or so before he seemed to realise the magnitude of his undertaking. Looking down the line he heaved a long, drawn-out sigh and exclaimed, "You Alabamians are the sickliest lot of soldiers it has ever been my misfortune to meet up with. What are you fellows up to anyhow?" Someone gave him a hint of our troubles, which aroused his sympathy, and he told us to go back to camp and that he would excuse the whole "lay-out". His report was sent up, stating that all the Alabama contingent of the 51st Tennessee was sick and not physically able for artillery service. That was the last we heard of "joining the artillery".

Shortly afterwards the 3rd Mississippi battalion, under Major Hardcastle, joined the army at Corinth. Along with some other loose companies of Mississippians not otherwise assigned to a particular command, we were thrown together and organised the 33rd Mississippi, afterwards the 45th Mississippi. We had at last found a home, as it were, and entered upon our duties with more spirit than at any time since we were recruited at Tuscumbia. Arms and accoutrements were issued to us, but the guns were old, clumsy, breech-loading affairs which had been thrown aside and probably rusting into the corner of some arsenal for years. However, we had no use for them, as long as we remained around Corinth, inactive, enlivened only occasionally by a skirmish between the pickets.*

Owing to bad sanitary conditions, miserable water, and probably other causes, our men began to get sick by the score. By the latter part of May, our regiment had 125 on the sick list, principally from Typhoid Fever. These were sent to hospitals at Columbus and other Mississippi towns, where many of them died. Others lingered through the summer months, recovering in time to join Gen. Bragg at Chattanooga during the latter part of August.

The Kentucky Campaign

During the spring, we evacuated Corinth and marched leisurely down to Tupelo, Mississippi, where we remained until July when camps were again broken and the main body of the army moved by rail to Chattanooga, preparatory to the invasion of Kentucky.

Nothing of special interest occurred during the few weeks we were around Chattanooga, but it was generally understood even by the privates that Kentucky was to be our destination. Accordingly, on August 28th 1862, we began crossing the Tennessee River, entering upon what proved to be a long and tiresome march.

We carried no tents, bivouacking anywhere we were allowed to stop long enough to get a few hours sleep, considering ourselves lucky if it happened to be in the timber where we could have the shelter of a tree. Nor were we burdened with baggage, as the Confederacy could not furnish us clothing and blankets, and having been cut off from home so long, what clothing we had was about worn out. In short, we started out "in light marching order", and held our own in that respect throughout the campaign.

---

* *The 33rd Mississippi was with the 16th Alabama, the 32nd Mississippi, the 44th Tennessee Regiments and Baxter's battery, brigaded under General S. A. M. Wood, in Hardee's Corps, June 30, 1862. Serial 10, page 786.*

The march through Tennessee was without hindrance except that we halted one day and two nights in Sequatchie Valley to give time for the artillery and wagon train, which was a long one, to cross the mountains. While here, the two Alabama companies got into trouble. Quite a number of boys from other regiments stole mules from the teamsters and rode out into the mountains foraging, and as it turned out to be, their forage consisted chiefly of apple brandy which was plentiful in that section.

After dark, Company K was detailed to picket the road on the mountain side, which was the only route for them to get back to camps. We had orders to arrest every man coming in, and before midnight, they began coming.

They came in squads of two, three, and four, and continued at intervals the remainder of the night, everyone having a jug or canteen full of apple brandy. By daylight, we had thirty or forty prisoners and as many gallons of "mountain dew". Prisoners, captors, officers, and privates all were in different stages of intoxication, a few drunk, but the majority of us had imbibed only enough to make us feel a little "boozy".

Alabamians in Trouble

When we reached camp, the rear of the army was just leaving and our division had been gone two hours, we followed, overtaking the command about noon, when the last one of us was very promptly placed under arrest and ordered to march in rear of the regiment. We found Company I (the other Alabama company) in the same fix for stealing "roasting ears" the day before. Corn, in the valley, was very fine and just in the right stage to be palatable, so the boys could not resist the temptation. After three days the privates were released and the commissioned officers continued under arrest until October 8th, when they were released to participate in the battle at Perryville.

We made a rapid march through Tennessee, crossing the Cumberland River (by wading) about sixty miles about Nashville, and reached Glasgow, Kentucky about September 10th, where General Bragg issued a proclamation, calling on Kentuckians to rally to his standard. He had been assured by citizens of the State that they would join the Confederacy if an opportunity was presented, and this was one of the objects of the invasion. Leaving Glasgow, we struck the Louisville and Nashville Railroad at Cave City in advance of General Buell who followed from Nashville.

Capture of Prisoners at Munfordsville

At Munfordsville, we thought we had "struck a snag" when we were drawn up where we could look into the muzzles of frowning guns and see the glistening arms of the infantry in the ditches, expecting every moment for the order to assault. We knew it would be a bloody affair, although we largely outnumbered the enemy, but the afternoon passed without orders and we slept on arms, dreading the light of day.

We were agreeably surprised when morning revealed white flags fluttering in the breeze, and the prisoners, 4000–5000, were marched out for our inspection. Besides prisoners we got a lot of arms, ammunition and other stores which we needed. The most important part of the capture, to us privates, being the hard tack and bacon which we were in fine condition to take care of. We tarried but a short time. Gathering up the spoils, we pushed on filing to the right towards Bardstown; General Buell passing our rear in the direction of Louisville.

At Bardstown we rested several days, the first rest we had had for about four weeks. We had been marching fifteen to twenty-five miles a day, on half rations of flour bread and bacon. The bread we had to cook at night after reaching camp, which was seldom earlier than midnight, when we were in the rear, and starting at 3:00 a.m. when we happened to be in front. The bacon we ate raw as it was too precious to waste any part of it in cooking, and almost any time during the campaign we could have eaten a day's rations at one meal.

Battle of Perryville

Our next point of interest after leaving Bardstown was Perryville, where we arrived on October 7th. The next day, while General Bragg was at Frankfort "inaugurating" a Confederate Governor, the booming of the guns cut short the ceremony and the Battle of Perryville was on.

This was a hard fought battle, and might be called a small one as compared with some others that were fought afterwards, but it seemed to us at the time to be a most tremendous affair and surely was a dangerous place as evidenced by the casualties of our two companies, which having been reduced from one cause or another to about seventy men, suffered a loss of eight killed and twenty-five wounded.

On our part of the line the battle began about noon. We were subjected to a most merciless shelling for about two hours, when we were ordered forward, and advancing within 200 or 300 yards of the enemy, halted and spread ourselves on the ground, and for another two hours we had an open field fight. Rather we were exposed in the open field while the enemy were posted on a hill among scattering timber which afforded them some protection with nothing to obstruct their view. It was a grand, but horrible, spectacle. When the dense smoke was lifted by a passing breeze, to witness the surging columns of gray and blue, which could be plainly seen a distance of one mile to the right. The firing was incessant and nothing but a continuous roar could be heard. If any commands were given, they could not be distinguished about the din. When it became necessary to move forward again, Colonel Charlton rode down the line and gave the command to each captain separately to, "fix bayonets, forward, double quick march." Up to this time our losses had been comparatively light, but when we raised the "rebel yell" and moved forward, it was then our boys were mowed down by the bullets of the Indianians on the hill.

General Wood, who commanded our brigade, was wounded early in the action by a piece of shell. In fact, almost every mounted officer in the brigade was either killed or disabled in the charge through the field. Our line had been very perceptibly thinned by the time we reached the foot of the hill, and the ascent was slow and laborious in the face of a terrible fire from an enemy two or three times our number. With all the advantage of position on their side we pressed on until within thirty yards of the top, when it seemed folly to attempt to go farther. A few began to waver, then more, and in a short time what was left of us descended the hill in about one fourth the time it required to cover the same distance on the advance. We retreated into the field but stopped behind the first ridge, which afforded any protection from the murderous fire which poured into us. We had hardly recovered "our breath" when a most thrilling and welcome sight greeted us—a long line of gray, General Polk's division coming to reinforce us.

We began to rally the stragglers and when General Polk's line reached us, we had thirteen of the two Alabama companies together under Lieutenant Bell Andrews, and falling in with them, moved forward again.

The Indianians stubbornly held their position, pouring deadly volleys into us, until it seemed that we would have to resort to the bayonet. To our relief, before the clash actually took place, they broke and fled precipitately from the field, leaving the dead and some of the wounded in our hands. Night had set in and a full October moon beaming down on the pale faces of the dead made it a ghastly spectacle to us, who had never witnessed anything like it before.*

Gathering Ammunition

We had used all our ammunition, and the ordnance train having left early in the morning, General Buckner ordered the Colonels to disband their regiments twenty minutes to supply ourselves from the cartridge boxes of the dead. They, too, had been using ammunition extensively and it was necessary for us to search many boxes before we got our own filled. We also exchanged many of our old guns for new Enfield rifles with which the enemy was armed. When we reformed our lines we hoped to go into camps, where we could rest and sleep the remainder of the night, but the army was already in motion and we had a tiresome night march till 1:00 a.m. when we bivouacked in a creek bottom where the timber had been cleared off and not a stick of wood left to make fires.

We had stripped our shirts for the fight and sent off blankets, coats and all baggage in the wagons that morning, not expecting to be caught out on a frosty night in such light apparel. The wagons were gone, we knew not where, and so exhausted with the day's battle and night's march, we were compelled to have

---

* *The statements made with regard to this battle are fully sustained by the report of General W. J. Hardee in Serial 22, pages 1119–1122.*

some sleep. Huddled together on the wet ground, we shivered and slept short naps until daylight.

We were not interrupted in our march to Camp "Dick Robinson" where we arrived on the tenth and remained the following day. While there, we were in the best of spirits and did not know that we were making preparations to retreat out of the state. Kirby Smith had whipped the Yankees at Richmond and we had whipped them at Perryville, and we thought General Bragg was only making a strategic move to take advantage of some other wind of the enemy's troops, "do them up", and drive the last one of them across the Ohio River, giving old Kentucky a chance to join the Confederacy.

A Disappointment—Short Rations & Hard Marching

On October 11th, we received orders to cook three days' rations and be ready to march at 3:00 a.m., which we presumed would be towards Cincinnati. During the night, however, the wagons and artillery began moving in the opposite direction and promptly at three o'clock the bugles sounded reveille and the head of the column followed in the wake of the wagons.

We soon "caught on" and realised that it was a retreat instead of an advance and that our Kentucky expedition was a failure. We had been in service about ten months and imagined we had seen some rough times, but this retreat proved to be the worst of our experience. By daylight we were strung out on the road towards Crab Orchard, and by noon had eaten the last of our three days' rations. Yet we were not full enough to impede locomotion in the least degree. We were not gluttonous either, as our three days' rations consisted of five biscuits and a small piece of bacon which was only an average breakfast for fellows who had been on half rations for the past month. We learned afterwards that hundreds of barrels of pickled pork had been destroyed after the soldiers had taken all they could carry, but it was where we did not have access to it and we knew nothing of it until too late to get our part. The day's march was made in "quick" time, with but few short stops for rest. The drought which had prevailed in this part of Kentucky during the fall caused the dust to be stifling and the scarcity of water added to our discomfort and to the fact of our failure to enlist recruits, which was one of the objects of this expedition. Being forced to abandon the beautiful bluegrass country preyed on our minds and made us feel despondent. The day's march was a hard one and we went into camps after midnight, so fatigued that it required but a short time for all of us to be sound asleep, forgetting our hunger and other troubles for a few short hours, and when bugles and drums roused us before daylight and we were off again; the pangs of hunger were not so acute on the second day as on the first. Before night we felt an "aching void" in our stomachs and a decided weakness in the lower extremities. On the second night we killed a few beeves, which after being divided we cut into strips, suspending them on ramrods before our camp fires to let them cook while we slept. Our jerked beef proved right savory, though without salt, and sustained us on the following day's march. We were sorely disappointed when night came and again we had no rations, except a few ears of corn we picked up during the day and parched in ashes. In the meantime the enemy was pressing us and the booming of the guns in the rear stimulated us to keep moving, consequently there was little straggling and no time for foraging.

Devouring a "Mudlark"

Late in the afternoon of the fifth day, we had the good fortune to run up on a fine, fat "mudlark"—commonly called a hog—which we killed and skinned. Dividing the meat we broiled it on the coals and devoured the whole of it before retiring for the night. After we got into the mountains we could not get even an ear of corn, as the land was too poor to raise anything more than a few "nubbins", and these the people had hid where a hungry rebel could not find them. The citizens here sympathized with the enemy and bushwhackers annoyed us from the mountain sides. At Wild Cat Pass, quite a squad of them screened behind a crag and in crevices above us, opened on us with squirrel rifles, creating some confusion in our ranks. Fortunately, no casualties resulted from it except a few slight wounds. Our march continued rapidly, considering our weakened condition from loss of sleep, long fasting, and being roused at 3:00 a.m., when in the front, and going into camps at midnight or after when in the rear.

We drew no rations until we arrived at Cumberland Gap on October 20th, where we got one fourth pound flour. This made two biscuits which we ate without salt or meat, just enough to wake up our stomachs and make us feel hungry again. For eight days we had not tasted bread nor had a spoonful of salt—salt, salt was the cry everywhere and a barrel of it could have retailed for a fortune—in Confederate money.

If plenty of provisions could have been provided it would not have been prudent to have issued full rations as we were in such a famished condition we would not have controlled our appetites, and the consequence might have seriously affected the efficiency of the army. We also got some tobacco here, which broke the famine from which we had suffered the past four or five weeks. We paid $2.50 each for six plugs of very poor quality, but it filled a "long-felt want" and was almost as much enjoyed as the two biscuits we had just eaten. Before leaving Chattanooga a few of the boys were wise enough to lay in a supply. A large majority of us however believed we were going into Kentucky where that article of luxury was supposed to be abundant and so deemed it useless to encumber ourselves with anything not absolutely necessary. Alas, when the small amount we carried in our pockets was gone we found it impossible to replenish. The merchants would not take our Confederate money and to conciliate the Kentuckians, General Bragg enforced the strictest discipline, giving us no opportunity of "foraging". For weeks there was no smoking around the camp fires and no chewing of the luscious weed while on the march.

From Cumberland Gap we got about one fourth rations and as the enemy had relaxed their pursuit we travelled more leisurely, arriving in Knoxville on the 25th in a dilapidated condition physically and otherwise. Since leaving Chattanooga, 55 days before, we had marched—including our meanderings—at least 600 miles. Most of those miles were accomplished on short rations, little sleep and only the "broad canopy of heaven" as our shelter. We had waded every stream from Chattanooga to near Louisville and from there back to Knoxville. Our clothing, well-worn from the start, was now in rags and tatters, shoes were worn out and many were entirely bare-footed, so when we awoke on the morning of the 26th and found four inches of snow on the ground and a cold wind blowing from the North, we felt that our lot had been cast in hard lines.

A Rest at Knoxville

We rested a few days at Knoxville and rations being a little more plentiful than we had been accustomed to for some time, we rapidly regained the flesh and strength that we had lost the preceding two weeks. In the meantime, General Rosecrans had superseded General Buell and was collecting a large army at Nashville. It became necessary for us to have one to oppose him; so we were loaded on freight trains and transferred as fast as possible to Chattanooga. From Chattanooga we had many delays on account of insufficiency of rolling stock of the railroad, but by marching and riding in turns we finally landed in front of the enemy, our division locating near Shelbyville on the bank of Duck River. While there, some of us enjoyed a visit from friends from home, who supplied us with much needed clothing and shoes. These items along with a limited number of tents having been issued, we were pretty well equipped for winter weather. Shortly after we got our camps adjusted we learned for the first time that the Camp Douglas prisoners had been exchanged and immediately sent up a petition that we be transferred to our regiment. In due time our request came back approved, accompanied by orders to report as soon as practicable at Port Hudson, Louisiana.

Port Hudson

We were hungry for sugar, having had none since we left Fort Henry in such haste ten months before. Gouging holes in the barrels and hogsheads we filled every receptacle we could command, but having left everything in Tennessee, except knapsacks and haversacks, we had few conveniences for carrying it. However, all made some shift: some wrapping it in dirty handkerchiefs, others in haversacks, and one fellow who happened to have an extra undergarment tied strings around the lower extremities, filled both legs with sugar and, when the boat came, slung it astride his shoulders and marched on to the amusement of the passengers and spectators. All of us were loaded with sugar and fairly revelled in sweetness all the way down the river. Little did we think that a few weeks from hence the very sight or smell of it would cause a heaving and a retching as will appear further on.

Reunion of the 27th Alabama

Our trip down the broad Mississippi was a very pleasant one, and about the middle of December we landed at Port Hudson, Louisiana. Port Hudson is a small town 25 miles above Baton Rouge. Here we found what was left of the 27th Alabama and it was both a sad and a pleasant meeting. There were absent many familiar faces of comrades who had succumbed to disease and given up their lives in prison and were perhaps buried in unmarked graves far away from home and loved ones who knew nothing of their fate. Having been exchanged three months before, the "balmy Southern breezes" had restored some to health, while others lingered and died from the effects of confinement and disease. The regiment was reorganized before our arrival, vacancies in field offices being

18

filled by promotion. Colonel Hughes having died, Lt. Col. James Jackson was promoted to Colonel; Maj. Edward McAlexander was promoted to Lieutenant Colonel; and Capt. R. G. Wright promoted to Major. Line offices were filled in the same way, which left some of the lieutenancies to be supplied by election.*

Although the climate was usually mild, winter had set in and frequent rains and cold winds from the North, to which we were exposed, rendered our situation very uncomfortable as we were not supplied with a sufficient number of tents to shelter us. Because of this, we began as soon as practicable to build houses for winter quarters. The only timber available was from the large stately bay trees which we cut and split and with the logs erected very respectable houses, which we covered with boards "chinking" the cracks with long hanging moss, which grew in abundance on the trees. We also built bunks and made beds of the same moss, and having swept off the streets, our camps presented an appearance quite cheerful, in striking contrast to what we had been accustomed.

Then began regular routine duties such as drilling, picket and guard duty, working on ditches, etc. Considerable work had been done on the fortifications, but they were far from complete, and a good portion of time was spent shovelling dirt, making a ditch seven feet deep and eight feet wide at the top, throwing the dirt inside for protection. The regiment, having been in prison almost from the beginning of enlistment, were naturally very deficient in the drill, consequently, a large part of the time was spent in this very necessary exercise. In the performance of all the duties devolving upon us we were kept very busily employed and had very little time for observing what was going on outside of our immediate vicinity.

Maj. Gen. Gardner was in command of our garrison consisting of 5000 or 6000 men, our line extending in a semicircle around the town, the flanks resting on the river above and below, while we had many pieces of artillery planted at intervals along the bank. Reinforcements were arriving almost every week during the winter until we were something like 15,000 strong. Alabama being represented by the 1st, 27th, 35th, 49th and 54th regiments and 4th Alabama battalion and possibly others. Frequent reports were brought by the cavalry that General Banks was advancing from Baton Rouge in large force, but these proved to be false alarms and resulted in nothing more than a formation in our respective positions which we held for a few hours and then marched back to camp.

Gray Backs

When we first rejoined the regiment, the camps were infested with gray backs which were very annoying and which we accused the boys of bringing

---

* The 27th Alabama was placed in General Beall's Brigade by General Orders, No. 5, Serial 21, page 934. On March 31 it appears in General A. Buford's brigade as appears from Serial 21, page 1033, The regiment under the command of Colonel James Jackson. Ed.

Douglas. After we got our houses completed and a few wash days, boiling and reboiling our clothing, blankets, etc., we got rid of the pests, proving the fallacy of what was often told for truth that "boiling water would not kill a body louse."

Much Sickness

Owing to bad water and detestable diet, we were soon stricken with a Dysentery which was very distressing and while a majority of us continued on duty, there were but few well men in the regiment during our four months stay. The writer was at this time clerk for the surgeon, whose duty it was to attend sick call, make a detailed report of the sick and then carry it to the Brigade surgeon. Long lines of sick were marched up to the Surgeon's tent every morning, and having noted for quite a while that the doctor prescribed Dover's powder in almost every case, with an occasional dose of Blue Mass, I asked him one morning why he prescribed the same medicine day after day. He replied, "It is the only medicine I have at all adapted to the prevailing disease. There are other remedies that would be much better in a large number of the cases, but I have none and they can not be procured." A small epidemic of Small Pox broke out during winter, but the cases were isolated to the 27th losing but one man. With this exception, and the Dysentery from which all of us suffered, we had but little sickness during our stay at Port Hudson.

Our rations from December to February consisted wholly of corn bread, blue beef, sugar and rice. The meal was the very coarsest and having no "sifter", except old tin pans with holes punched in them, it was impossible to make good bread of it. The beeves were so poor they could scarcely walk, and a whole day's boiling would not raise an "eye" of grease in the pot. Driven from Texas, poor when they started, they were in a starving condition when they reached us. The sugar was of the wet, brown variety and we had been surfeited on it until the very sight of it was nauseating, and it emptied on the hill side by the kettle full every morning. The rice was palatable at first but got to be as offensive as the sugar. All taken together, the rations were so repugnant we could barely eat enough to sustain life, but on the 24th of February a steamer arrived from Red River loaded with hogs, bacon and corn, which caused great rejoicing. The good news was carried from regiment to regiment and yells from thousands of throats rent the air from one end of the line to the other. We had been praying for months for something to eat and old bacon was the most desirable of anything which we had hopes of getting. This unexpected addition to our rations was a godsend, as our health began to improve immediately. With our returning strength we felt more like meeting the advance of Gen. Banks, which we had every reason to believe would take place within a short time.

During all the winter we had to do all our washing with plain water, no soap having been issued for many months, and all the beeves killed at Port Hudson would not have made enough tallow to make a pound of soap. After rations began to come in, "grease" was a little more plentiful and details were made to cut timber, burn and use the ashes for making lye soap, and then we had the satisfaction of wearing clean clothes once more.

Our River Navy

The fleet remained in the river below, usually very quiet, but at intervals throwing a few shells by way of diversion. No attempt was made to pass our batteries, as was the case at Vicksburg. Frequently, gunboats would try to float by the latter place in the darkness, but were usually discovered in time and driven back. However, the *Indianola*, one of the most powerful gunboats of the Federal navy, succeeded in running the gauntlet and caused consternation among our steam boats, which plied between the two fortified places and an expedition was planned for her capture or destruction.

Accordingly on February 14th, a call was made for volunteers, we were drawn up in line, the object stated, and we were warned to consider well, as it was a perilous undertaking and there must be no flinching when the ordeal came. We were limited to one man from each company, but when the command was given, many more than were needed to fill our quota stepped to the front. Then it was decided to determine by lot who should go. Ten men were thus selected to represent the 27th Alabama, and I regret very much that I can not give their names; Ike Landers of Company C being the only one I can recall at this time.

The *Dr. Beatty*, a large transport, was armored for the expedition, fortified with cotton bales from stem to stern, with port holes for the guns. On the 16th, our "volunteer tars" boarded her, and gallantly steamed up the river, cheered by the thousands of officers and soldiers who had congregated on the bank to witness our departure. Days of suspense followed, we could hear nothing authentic from the expedition, fears and hopes alternated. After a time, reliable news was received that the boys had found the object of their quest at or near Gordon's Landing in Red River, and after a sharp engagement she had surrendered with 98 men and everything on board, with the loss to us of two killed and four wounded.

Contrary to expectation, the winter wore away and March came without any general engagement, but the fleet entertained us in a more lively manner by "pitching" over a few large shells every day and occasionally by a severe bombardment of an hour or more duration, but with slight casualties on our side. Our batteries made no reply, preferring to keep the enemy in ignorance of their location until the struggle should come on in earnest. We continued strengthening our works, and made details from each regiment to construct rafts for the purpose of obstructing the river below our batteries to prevent the passage of boats.

When opportunity presented, which was not often the case, we delighted in going down to look at the boats composing the fleet. We had never seen any frigates and "men of war" and it was a great sight to us. We could crawl up to the banks, taking care not to expose ourselves to view, and on one occasion I made a memorandum of names as follows: Flagships *Hartford, Mississippi, Richmond, Monongahela*; gunboats *Kineo, Essex, Tennessee, Brooklyn, Pensacola, Albatross, Sachem*. Besides these, five mortar boats were stationed in a bend of the river below the fleet.

Payne Money

On the 1st day of March, we "mustered for pay". We had not been paid for many months and money was scarce, but we had a resourceful member of the regiment who relieved the stringency by supplying a circulating medium which answered the purpose to some extent. This individual was known throughout the army as R. E. Payne, "The Banker". He was not as "green" as he looked to be nor, as one would suppose, to be a man who had lived forty years in the Sand Mountains of North Alabama. He was a great forager and trader: he bought and sold for profit anything a soldier could use, from a pint of Louisiana rum to a bed quilt or a mess of potatoes. He had followed trafficking ever since he enlisted in the army, but was accumulating wealth too slowly for a man of his business capacity. He conceived the idea of adding a banking business, and accordingly got a printer to print for him several thousand dollars of "money" in several denominations ranging from fifty cents to ten dollars. It read "Redeemable in Confederate money when presented in sums of $20.00 and upwards—signed R.E. Payne." Whether he bought or sold "promised to pay" was current, it was seldom refused, so Payne turned the bulk of his money into Confederate and was just "rolling" in wealth. He had the Confederate and we the "Payne Money".

He made good his promise and redeemed all that was presented according to the printed terms, but it was not often that any of us had as much as $20.00 at one time, and when we did have to take up a batch of it, he passed it on to the next fellow and kept it in circulation.

Early in March we received reinforcements, increasing our effective force to 10,000–12,000 men. We were in good spirits and eager for the fray, our works in good shape, we felt confident that we could hold them against any land force that might be brought against us, provided our river batteries were able to hold back the fleet and prevent the passage of boats up the river. The enemy was reported advancing in strong force from Baton Rouge. Pickets were doubled, unusual activity of couriers and staff officers, all indicated that we might expect stormy times very soon, but with the exception of a few false alarms, and the shelling from the fleet sometimes in a slow good-natured way, then a furious bombardment for an hour or more, nothing of interest occurred until March 14th.

Battle of Port Hudson

It was a lovely day, the air cool and pleasant, birds singing, woods green and all nature looked bright and cheerful. The fleet was quietly anchored in its accustomed position, and all remained calm until 2:00 p.m. when without warning—boom! boom! boom! the big shells came screeching through the camps. The long roll was beaten and hastily forming line we double-quicked to our positions behind the breastworks. No enemy in sight, we had nothing to do but watch the bursting shells and curling smoke, which in the bright sunlight made a beautiful appearance. Out breastworks were no protection as the boats were almost on a line with us, and although many shells burst near by we escaped without a casualty. The bombardment continued incessantly for about three hours, when it ceased and all was quiet again, but the land forces were reported to be near and advancing, so we had to remain in position and were ordered to "sleep on arms." Spreading our blankets on the ground, we lay down and one by one we dropped off until all but the sentries pacing their boats were perhaps dreaming sweet dreams of peace and happiness with loved ones at home. These dreams were destined to be rudely disturbed, for just at eleven o'clock the thunder guns broke the stillness of the night air and startled us from our slumbers. It was not necessary for our drummer to beat his long roll, every man was at his post in an instant thinking this was a signal for an attack by land, which we awaited rather anxiously feeling confident that we could repel any assault that might be made. Owing to neglect or other cause the piles of fagots which had been prepared for the purpose of illuminating the river in case of a night attack were not lighted and our artillerists were deprived of the advantage it would have afforded them. Nevertheless, they replied promptly and the continuous thunder of several hundred guns, the comet-like fuses of large shells as they darted through the darkness,

23

the mortar shells rising high up in the heavens, descending like "shooting stars", bursting and scattering fragments in every direction, presented the grandest and most exciting exhibition of fireworks that we had ever witnessed.

The boats made many attempts to pass, but our gallant artillerists poured such a storm of shot and shell into them that they were compelled to retire each time, some of them so crippled that they floated off helplessly down the river.

After three hours of incessant firing two gunboats succeeded in running the gauntlet and the frigate *Mississippi* seemed in a fair way to go by, but when opposite our batteries the boys poured such a stream of "hot shot" into her side that she was disabled, on fire and floated off downstream. Then the rebel yell, long and loud, was carried down the line from one end to the other.

The burning ship illuminated the country for miles around, and for fear of a general conflagration the rest of the fleet withdrew before her. She continued floating down the river, her bombs bursting and loaded guns shooting as the fire reached them, until just as day began to dawn a tremendous explosion shook the earth and her remains went to the bottom of the river. (The now famous Admiral George Dewey was Executive officer on this ship.)

The enemy was completely foiled, their intention being to run enough boats by our batteries to have a fleet above and below, so they could shell us from both sides, while the infantry attacked us in front. The disabling of so many boats and the burning of the frigate caused such consternation among them that they (the infantry) retreated in haste to Baton Rouge. Our loss was very light, though the artillerists suffered more than we, as they bore the brunt of the battle with the fleet while the mortar boats directed their attention to us in the trenches. It seems almost incredible that such a terrific bombardment of three hours duration, when the elements were filled with flying missiles weighing from 100 to 400 pounds bursting and scattering fragments everywhere, should result in such small loss of life.

After the Battle

We spent the remainder of the night without sleep, listening to the boom of the guns and shells on the *Mississippi* and watching the flashes produced by the explosives, wondering what would come next. It began to rain early in the morning and having no shelter, we were soon drenched, but had to make the best of it until about noon when two-thirds of the regiment were marched back to camps to prepare something to eat for themselves and the unfortunates who were left in the trenches.

The fleet resumed its old position in line of battle and reminded us of its presence by an occasional shot, but showed several vacant places in its formation. The *Mississippi, Monongahela, Richmond* and *Ganessee* were absent but so far as we could discern, the others were in fighting condition and as the land forces had retired from our front we felt confident there would be no general engagement at least for some time to come. Consequently, we took up our regular routine duties, interrupted only by bombardments of more or less severity, sometimes opening on us at midnight or other unreasonable hour, much to our discomfort and disturbance of rest.

Since we had a change in our rations a great improvement was discernible in that our physical condition, health and strength had returned and the morale of the army was better than it had been all winter. We had become so disgusted with rice and sugar that for some time we refused to take it off the commissary's hands, but good old bacon and cornbread seemed to be the very diet we needed and this was all we got except occasionally when some good "forager" would dodge the guards and buy, beg or steal a mess of vegetables from one of the neighboring planters. On March 26th beef with fat on it was issued to us, the first of the kind we had seen since we left the army of Tennessee and it also proved to be the last during our stay at Port Hudson. Where it came from we never knew but we had about come to the conclusion that there was not a cow in Louisiana fat enough to make a tallow candle. We saved the fat, borrowed molds from a citizen and made tallow candles which we used for lighting purposes at night, a luxury we had not enjoyed for quite a long while.

About this time some of the boys who had been home on furlough returned and brought us letters from friends and sweethearts. It was very seldom we got any news from home especially Companies C, E and I, which were made up in the counties north of the Tennessee River. As the river was the dividing line between the Confederates and Federals all mails had been discontinued since early in 1862. Occasionally someone would slip through the lines and, if fortunate enough to escape capture, would come out loaded with letters. In this way all our correspondence was carried on and it was only at intervals, and often long ones, that we could hear from friends or they from us.

Leaving Port Hudson

April brought no change in the situation, the land forces remained quiescent at Baton Rouge, the fleet anchored in the river below, now and then shelling the woods or throwing a few shells into our camps, but we had become so accustomed to them, and they did so little harm, that we hardly noticed them except on occasions when the cannonading was unusually heavy. Rumors spread through the camps that we would soon leave Port Hudson for a field of greater activity, but were not confirmed until the morning of the 6th.* We were ordered to cook rations, pack up and be ready to move at a moment's notice. The order was received with cheers, but at the same time we felt some degree of sadness at the

* *See Serial 21, page 1037.* Ed.

thought of leaving a place where we were so comfortably quartered. We had our houses in splendid condition, many little conveniences arranged for our comfort and we had been here so long it seemed almost like home. Besides, we were at last getting very fair rations and taken all together were having about as good times as a soldier could expect. But inactivity begets restlessness and the constant drill, guard and fatigue duty had become monotonous and we were willing to make a change. While we might expect harder and possibly more dangerous service than we had seen the past few months.

Cooking rations required but a short time and as to "packing", it was a small job having no tents and nothing to pack except our scanty knapsacks. By 10 o'clock we were bidding farewell to the comrades who had to remain and took up the line of march towards Clinton, 25 miles distant, at which town we arrived the next afternoon. We left Clinton early on the 8th and went into camps at 3 p.m. on the banks of Amite river, a very pretty stream where we had much fun bathing and swimming mules. On the 9th and 10th we marched 30 miles to Osyka, Mississippi, a town on the N.O.J. and Great Northern Railroad as it was then known, where we expected to take a train for Jackson.

From some cause we were delayed three days but had no reason to complain on that account, as we were not subjected to strict discipline and had a delightful time with the many pretty girls of the town, attended Sunday School and Church, a privilege we had not enjoyed in so long a time we hardly knew how to conduct ourselves properly.

While there, a member of the regiment received his discharge for disability and we utilized the opportunity of writing letters to homefolk, friends and sweethearts and when they were collected the poor fellow was almost overwhelmed with mail.

April 13th we boarded a freight train for Jackson, every car packed full and tops thick as blackbirds, the rain pouring down drenched those on top while the occupants on the inside were crowded almost to suffocation. Reaching Jackson at dark, we marched out two miles through mud and rain and had to bivouac without tents. It was so dark we could see nothing and everything was so wet we could not make fires. We spent a miserable night, wrapped only in our blankets, exposed to the rain which fell in torrents the whole night. The next day continued rainy but on the following day the clouds were dispersed and we dried ourselves in the sunshine having had a thorough soaking of 48 hours.

Ordered to Army of Tennessee

April 16th we got orders, which were not unexpected, to report to General Bragg and forthwith started on another freight but were sidetracked sixty miles from Jackson, where we remained all night, took a fresh start, ran to Meridian and stopped for another night. On the 18th we left Meridian at 4:00 a.m., bowled along at the rate of five miles per hour to Selma. Our slow progress was discouraging and we thought if General Bragg needed reinforcements very much, he would be sorely disappointed however, we were enjoying the trip for the ladies met us at every station, cheering us, not only with their smiles and showering upon us bouquets of fragrant flowers, but with more solid comforts in the shape of something to eat.

At Selma we took the steamer, *Henry J. King*, and made a night run to Montgomery, arriving there the next morning. On landing guards were placed and orders issued for all to remain on board. "What does it mean?", was asked by everyone, but we soon learned that it meant orders were countermanded and we were to go back to Mississippi! We had our "heads set" to go back to Tennessee to breathe the mountain air and slake our thirst in the clear springs and streams of that region and it was a great disappointment to be compelled to turn back. A large force under General Grant was concentrating in the vicinity of Vicksburg and I presume the authorities deemed the reinforcement of General Bragg of less importance than the assistance we could render our little army in Mississippi.

The return trip was slow but after two days of hard pulling we landed in Meridian where the brigade was stopped and the 27th Alabama proceeded on to Big Black River, 18 miles east of Vicksburg.* Arriving at our destination in the night our train was stopped in a dense wood. Nobody was there to show us where to go, a severe storm of rain, thunder and lightning was raging and it was so dark it was impossible to see anything except by the flashes of lightning. The Colonel was despairing of ever getting us into anything like decent order, so gave the command "break ranks and look out for yourselves." Each fellow struck out on his own hook, hunting for a dry place on which to roost, but none of us were fortunate enough to find it. The rain continued to pour down all night and when daylight came our drummer was beating his drum at a fearful rate in an endeavor to assemble the boys who were scattered all over the bottom. While this was going on the Colonel was looking for a suitable location in which to camp and when he did we found it was an ideal place.

Large oaks furnished plenty of shade, wood was abundant and convenient and a fine spring of clear, cold water bubbled up in the edge of the camp. Towards the middle of the day the sun shone out and, spreading our wet clothing and blankets on the bushes to dry, all of us plunged into the river to take a bath. At first we were a little shy of alligators which infested the stream, but if any ugly reptiles had been inclined to make a dinner off one or more of us, the noise we made yelling and splashing in the water was enough to scare him off. At any rate we were not molested.

The 27th Alabama were the only troops at the bridge the first week, but on the 28th we were reinforced by the 19th Arkansas. On the 30th four more regiments came in and the following day General Tilghman with his brigade and we

* See Serial 38, page 805. Ed.

began fortifying all approaches to the bridge. This made quite a formidable force for defense, but it soon became necessary to send part of it to reinforce General Bowen at Grand Gulf who was engaged with one of General Grant's flanking columns.

For several days, while busily employing ourselves with pick and spade, we could hear the storm of battle at Grand Gulf and Port Gibson, but after desperate and stubborn resistance General Bowen was compelled to retreat and the head of his column arrived on May 4th. Two days later all had come in and they were assigned to positions, with us, for protection of the bridge. Meanwhile, fighting and heavy cannonading was of daily occurrence in the vicinity of Vicksburg. It looked as if we were getting into a close place: a victorious army below; a large force in our front, and still another in the vicinity of Yazoo City, which was liable to come in our rear; however, we were much encouraged by reports of success at Vicksburg, but more so by the trainload of troops which were passing us every day and pouring into the beleaguered city. We hoped to be able to collect an army sufficient to meet General Grant on something like an equal footing, and in that case felt confident in our ability to defeat him, but how our hopes were blasted will appear further on.

On May 6th, we were ordered to send everything that could be dispensed with to Vicksburg. Our brigade came in about the same time and we were right glad to see them. We had been astray three weeks, but had a good time eating wild honey and drinking buttermilk. "Bee trees" were numerous in the bottom and many large trees were felled and the quantity of honey we got from some of them was enormous. Our supply of buttermilk came from a good lady, a wealthy widow, who owned a large cotton plantation near the camps. Having learned that we were North Alabamians, and being originally from that section of the state, she naturally felt more interest in us than in the other troops and told us to come every morning as long as we were in reach of her. She had thirty or forty cows and a great many slaves who attended to the milking and churning and we got the whole output of buttermilk while the poor little pickaninnies suffered for their usual supply. Buttermilk and honey were rarities in our bill of fare and, together with our regular rations, we fared sumptuously during our three weeks' stay near Big Black Bridge.

An "Oyster Stew"

There were a great many mussels in the river and, as they resembled oysters very much, we could see no reason why they would not make a good stew. While we were bathing, we gathered up bushels of fine, large ones and soon had an extra large kettle boiling. At intervals we fished for an "oyster" to see whether it was getting tender, but every time with the same result: it was as tough as leather. Every hour's boiling seemed to make them tougher, until finally we got discouraged and gave it up. We were not wholly disappointed, however as we had twelve gallons of soup which was really palatable.

The week from May 6th to 18th was marked by a good deal of activity of the forces on both sides. A large force of the enemy crossed the river above us and moved in the direction of Jackson, while another was coming from Grand Gulf and we expected this detachment to attempt a crossing below.

Having sent all our surplus baggage to Vicksburg our brigade was ordered to cook rations and be ready to march at a minute's warning, but just as we had our biscuit dough made up we had to "fall in" and move out in quick time towards Grand Gulf. We marched until midnight and bivouacked in line. The next day we were ordered to cook rations again and in a short time had our sourdough, which we carried in haversacks, as well as the additional rations which we received, cooked and ready for orders again. The brigade remained in bivouac. The 27th was ordered to the front on picket, taking position where the enemy was expected to cross. They were there in considerable force on the opposite side of the little river but remained quietly on their own side and we had no disposition to start a "fuss" with them in as much as they made no effort to cross. We remained on picket during the day and night and on the morning of the 10th found the enemy had disappeared from our front and had crossed the river below us, leading us to follow in their rear. For three days we maneuvered in close proximity to them, but too weak to offer battle, contented ourselves with skirmishing and watching their movements.

While we were following and harassing this column of the enemy, the large force aforementioned were moving eastward threatening Jackson and other interior towns. Orders were dispatched to us by courier to return to the bridge with all possible haste. Arriving there at midnight of the 18th, we slept two or three hours when the "long roll" called us into line before daylight. We hastened to our temporary breastworks, thinking the enemy was upon us and at last we would have the opportunity of defending the bridge, which we had been guarding for some weeks, but not so. The army was already in motion and about eight or nine o'clock we fell in the rear leaving only a small force at the bridge.

Having marched about four miles the 27th and one other regiment were formed in line of battle near the intersection of two roads to intercept a raiding party of cavalry, while the army continued on the march. The raiders took another route and we were not molested, but remained in this position, expecting them all the time, for two days and nights. During this time we were exposed to heavy rains for which we were not at all prepared having sent everything to Vicksburg, except the clothing we wore. On the 15th we were relieved from our position at the crossroads and after a very hard day's march overtook the command in the afternoon. About dark we halted for the night in a clearing where there were great piles of dead timber and brush just ready for the match, as if they had been prepared for our special benefit. In a little time we had bright fires burning which illuminated the surrounding country and everything looked so cheerful we forgot our fatigue from the day's march. We spent the early part of the night singing, laughing and yelling; the merriest time we had had in many days. We had been under the impression for several days that we were in close proximity to the enemy and that a battle was imminent, but when we were allowed to build fires of such huge proportions and observing the lack of usual precautions when in the presence of the enemy, we concluded this might be only a feint and possibly the Yankees had retired to Vicksburg.

I have heretofore neglected to mention that when we arrived at Jackson we were assigned to Loring's division, Buford's brigade, the division being composed of Featherstone's, Adam's and Buford's brigades. Our brigade had nine regiments as follows: 27th, 35th, 49th, and 54th Alabama; the 12th Louisiana; the 9th Arkansas; and the 3rd, 7th and 8th Kentucky.

Battle of Baker's Creek or Champion Hill

On May 16, 1863, while we were breakfasting on the remnants of our scanty rations, a sudden volley of artillery in our immediate front announced to us that the Yankees were much nearer to us than we had imagined the night before. It was a genuine surprise to us if not to our commanders and subsequent events tended to confirm our opinion that there was a failure somewhere to realize the situation as it was. Unexpected as it was we had no confusion, but activity was apparent all over the camps in an instant and it required but a few moments to don our accoutrements and be ready for orders.

We were hastily thrown into line of battle, our division (Loring's) constituting the right wing, Browne's division the left and Stephenson's division the centre. Skirmishing began at once continuing for about an hour when we fell back for a better position. The enemy moved up promptly and a lively skirmishing again ensued. General Bowen was hotly engaged on the left, still we remained in position until 2 o'clock when we were ordered to the scene of action. We double-quicked, it seemed to us, at least three miles under a blistering sun, with not a drop of water in our canteens. When we reached the battle field we were almost exhausted, but dashed into the fray with cheers and yells to encourage our boys who by that time were slowly falling back. Stimulated by our presence some of them rallied and the battle raged furiously again.

Several of our regiment were killed or wounded before we fired a gun and at about this time General Tilghman was killed by a cannon shot. We held them in check while Bowen's and Stephenson's divisions were thrown against the enemy's right wing to open up a way for retreat. They succeeded in securing possession of the Vicksburg road, which they followed, leaving us entirely cut off from the remainder of the army. It has been said that General Loring was

31

ordered to follow the other two divisions but refused. Whether this be true or not, we were left to confront an overwhelming force and it was soon apparent, even to us privates, that we were whipped and must either retreat or surrender.

As rapidly as possible, General Loring drew off his command our brigade protecting the rear and, by forming successive lines of battle wherever the nature of the ground gave us an advantage, we held the victorious Federals in check until the division was in full retreat. Being cut off from all roads we were compelled to take to the woods and fields and, pressed on flanks and rear, it was expedient to abandon wagons, artillery and everything which tended to impede our retreat and even with no encumbrances it seemed like escape would be impossible. About sundown the division, all except our regiment which was the extreme rear, had succeeded in passing through the field into a dense wood. Unfortunately, the head of the column had struck a swamp, causing a blockade, so that we could not move forward without breaking ranks which we felt very much inclined to do and required all the "grit" we possessed to resist. The rear of the regiment kept pressing forward until we were jammed up in a solid mass, exposed to the fire of ten times our number. It seemed for a time that annihilation was to be our fate, but the distance proved to be greater than in our excited state of mind we had imagined and many of the shots fell short, though quite a number of the regiment were left on this part of the field.

After a time, which to us seemed a long one, the column ahead of us managed to stretch out giving us room to show our speed in a race for the timber— which we reached just as the yelling, surging masses were closing in on us from flank and rear.*

Once in the timber we were out of their clutches for the time and welcomed the night soon spreading her mantle around us, effectually concealing us from our bloodthirsty pursuers. We were in an unknown forest without a road or star to guide us, almost surrounded by a foe flushed with victory, wagons and artillery captured and no rations in our haversacks. Staff officers were stationed on the line of march, warning us not to speak above a whisper, as we were passing between two bodies of the enemy. Their camp fires were burning brightly on both sides of us and we steered as nearly as possible between them and no doubt it was largely due to this that we were enabled to make our escape, for without the lights for a guide we would probably have wandered right into their camps. Slowly and silently as a funeral procession we groped our way through

---

* General Buford's report of the Battle of Baker's Creek in Serial 37, page 87, says: "I was more than gratified at the gallant bearing of the commanding officers, as well as that of the other field and company officers. To say that I am proud to command the brigade evinces but slightly the high regard and estimation I have for the troops. Their quickness of motion, their ardor, powers of endurance, and steadiness exhibited during the engagement of Saturday and on the retreat are worthy of mention." His report notices the death on the field of Captain W. A. Isbell, Company G, and Lieutenant T. S. Taylor of Company I, 27th Alabama. Ed.

woods and fields and swamps until midnight when, considering ourselves reasonably safe, the restrictions were removed and we discussed the events of the day, our hazardous retreat and marvelous escape. The opinion was generally expressed that General Pemberton must have handled his troops very badly, his criticism of the operations of a large body of troops is not entitled to much consideration. No doubt we were largely out-numbered, but it did seem to us that if good generalship had been displayed we should have been able to retreat in order and with much less loss than we sustained.

The march was slow and laborious, the night being so dark we could only feel our way through the thickets and underbrush. When we would come into open fields we could see our file leaders and follow with more ease. Without a single stop we pressed forward all night and daylight Sunday morning, May 17th, found us still plodding along, hungry, weary and sleepy with no prospect for food or rest.*

At sunrise we stopped long enough to call the roll and ascertained that about one third of the regiment was missing. Of Company C 34 men went into the fight and 22 answered to their names (3 sergeants and 9 privates missing) and I presume about the same proportion held in the other companies. At that time we had no means of knowing the respective numbers of the killed, wounded or captured, but learned afterwards that quite a goodly number of them were prisoners, and our list of casualties was smaller than we had reason to fear it was. After thirty minutes rest we moved on and "dragged one foot after the other" going into bivouac at sundown, having been on foot thirty-six hours without food and had to go to sleep supperless. Having stacked arms, we threw ourselves on the ground without even a blanket to shield us from the night dew, or a knapsack for a pillow and in a very few moments the whole division was sleeping so soundly that the explosion of a sixty pound bomb shell would hardly have awakened us.

No enemy being near it is needless to say we got a full night's sleep, but arose the next morning stiff and footsore. We drew a small ration of beef without salt or bread, which we broiled on the coals and ate at one meal relieving to some extent the "gnawing at the stomach" which a fast of 48 hours had produced. We rested till 11:00 a.m., then tramped 13 miles to Pearl River where we camped again without supper. Here we learned for the first time that a large force of the enemy had captured and sacked the city of Jackson a few days before.

The next morning we drew bacon and meal from which the commissary had "presses" in the country. This was the first food we had had for three days, except the small ration of beef on the day before, but there was not a cooking vessel of any description in the brigade, so we had to make up our dough on boards, pieces of bark or any flat material we could procure. Probably more "ashcakes" were made in one hour than had ever been made in the same length

---

* See Buford's report in Serial 37, pages 82–87. Ed.

of time and everybody knows they are hard to beat for bread, but I made an improvement on the style of cooking mine without the unpleasant feature of having it coated with ashes. I found a corn shuck from which the ear had been removed and, making up my dough on a broad piece of bark, filled the shuck, tying the end with hickory bark, covered it with hot ashes and coals. My experiment proved a complete success, for when I uncovered it and stripped off the shuck, I had a beautiful "pone" of bread just the size and shape of an ear of corn and I can truthfully say it was the best bread I have ever eaten before or since.

So much invigorated by the delicious bread and bacon, we were enabled to make a fair day's march, and the following day arrived in Jackson at 2:00 p.m., finding the city in ruins. What a contrast compared with what it was only a short time ago when we were there. The enemy had destroyed the government works, public buildings, warehouses, depots and much private property. A great many citizens had fled from their homes and the city looked desolate and forsaken. We halted but a short time and moved out on the Canton road four miles to a creek where we pitched camp. Here we drew one day's rations, one pot to each company and one over (without a lid) to two companies, a slim showing for cooking indeed, but we didn't have much to cook.

We remained very quietly in this camp for about a week, the only excitement being the cannonading at Vicksburg which was almost constant day and night. The force which we fought at Baker's Creek followed Bowen and Stephenson to Vicksburg and together with the army already there made the investment of the city complete and assaults on some part of the line were of daily occurrence in all of which our boys were victorious. A number of our regiment who were sick and on detached duty at the time of the battle fell in with the retreating army and went into Vicksburg. Almost every day one or more of them returned to us having slipped through the lines at night and all their reports were encouraging.

General Johnston

On May 26th we were inspected by General Joseph E. Johnston, who had taken command of the department a short time previously. He was received with prolonged cheers, his presence infused renewed confidence in our little command and as reinforcements were coming we felt with him to lead us we might soon attack Grant in the rear, raise the siege and relieve the garrison at Vicksburg.

We spent the latter part of May and a large portion of June roaming around in the vicinity of Canton, Yazoo City and Big Black River, expecting every day to move on Vicksburg. Occasionally halting a few days, when our time was employed in drilling, inspection and other duties which served the purpose of keeping us out of mischief, to some extent, but it was impossible to make all of us good all of the time. The boys would "forage" for something to eat, regardless of orders to the contrary. On the night of June 15th some of the boys who were out on a "scout" captured a bee gum and detailed Monroe Cothran to carry it to camp. The night was pitch dark and Monroe, stumbling into a ditch, busted the gum causing the bees to cover him and soon made it so hot he abandoned his prize and struck a "bee line" for camp. Not a handsome boy at best, the next morning he was in a pitiable plight. His freckled face and red head swollen to enormous proportions, he was the most hideous looking human imaginable. He told the captain a spider bit him and the Captain, thinking it must have been a very venomous spider, sent for the surgeon who evidently had doubts in his mind, gave Monroe the benefit of the doubt, so the officers remained in ignorance of the true cause.

During most of the month of June, the weather was hot and sultry, rendering our marches from one point to another very disagreeable. The dust, shoe mouth deep, stirred by horses, wagons and artillery was so dense we couldn't see ten feet before us. We perspired and wiped our faces with dirty hands, the dust continually accumulating until the skin was covered with a thick coat, so masked our features that we could not recognize our most intimate chum. Our mouths, noses and throats were so stifled with it that we could scarcely breathe. In addition to this, water was scarce and part of the time ponds were the only accessible sources of supply and these were often stirred by hundreds of beef cattle and so hot it almost scalded the throat when swallowed. Another serious problem we had to contend with was the scarcity of cooking utensils, the whole regiment having no more than one company needed. Cooking by turns and disputing about whose time came next, usually the night was well spent before we got our rations prepared and consequently we felt little like marching the next day.

We had drawn no clothing for quite a long time and, as might be supposed, were a ragged set, with the exception of a few of us who were fortunate enough to have some sent from home. On June 17th the Quartermaster informed us he had received a supply and the announcement was received with demonstrations of joy, but after an inventory of his stock was taken, and a division among the companies completed, it was disappointing. A memorandum of Company C's share will give a fair idea of what the regiment got, as the goods were as nearly equally divided as was possible.

Company C had forty men present and its prorata was five pairs of cotton pants, six shirts, one pair of drawers. The pants and shirts were issued to those who needed them most, but it was a hard matter to decide as all were in about the same fix. When it came to the solitary garment, it was suggested to "draw straws" for them. All who were entirely destitute were ordered into line and fourteen responded. One long and thirteen short straws were prepared and the lottery declared open for business. The drawing then proceeded with much merriment, for the spectators, resulting in the capital prize being won by Dick Terrill.

For five or six weeks we had been wandering around in the territory between Canton and the Big Black, never more than 20 or 30 miles from a central point. In the meantime the thunder of the guns day after day and night after night told us that the heroic little city was still victorious and encouraged us with the hope that she would be able to hold out until we could collect a force sufficient to render assistance. We were fully aware of the strength of the enemy and realized that we could accomplish nothing without a desperate struggle, but had all confidence in General Johnston and believed that when the auspicious moment arrived he would lead us to victory. In all our meanderings only at one time did we cross the river, and then we thought the time had come to make the attempt to raise the siege and relieve the starving garrison, but it turned out to be only a reconnoitering expedition. We constructed an "imitation" pontoon bridge by felling the tall trees from both sides of the river, lapping the tops in the middle of the stream, placing large posts for supports, then laying the floor on these, which made us a very respectable bridge. We then marched over, stacked arms and rested while the cavalry, under General W. H. Jackson, crossed and passed on to the front.

As our bridge was a little shaky and not capable of sustaining great weight, the boys had to ride in a thin line and took up so much time, it was 5:00 p.m. when the last one reached the west side of the river. We had much fun guying the "critter companies" as was always the case when cavalry and infantry were thrown together. Such foolishness as the following was indulged in the whole time they were passing:

"Where are you going, boys?"

"Going to Vicksburg."

"Well, let us know when you start back, so we can get out of your way."

"Say boys, don't pop any more caps."

"Why?"

"Oh, you might scare these fellows and cause a stampede!"

Of course this was all for fun, we knew the cavalry were indispensable and composed of the same material as the "web feet" as they called us. Soldiers will have fun at somebody's expense and it seemed natural for cavalry and infantry to have a tilt whenever they met, but when the tug of war came, each had a part to perform and valued the other's assistance. The cavalry out of the way, we moved on six miles and bivouacked in line.

The next day, five miles further, but this was the last advance towards Vicksburg. We remained in the swamps two or three days, recrossed the river and pitched camps at Moore's Ferry where we remained a few days and had brigade review. A great many citizens were out to view the parade and General Buford being somewhat of a ladies man got up a sham battle for their entertainment. It was a hot day and we double-quicked, yelled, and charged the Pointe Coupee battery all the afternoon, until we were ready to drop from exhaustion. It was fun for the General and spectators, but we didn't enjoy it "a little bit."

When we left this camp, we marched back in the direction of Canton and, while in camp at the Fulton farm, some friends from North Alabama arrived with a large quantity of clothing and letters. The ladies at home had sewing societies, wove and made clothing, knitted socks, scraped lint, etc. and when opportunity presented, sent us the fruit of their labors. The clothing came at an opportune time as we had sent everything to Vicksburg almost three months before and never expected to see them again. We had heard nothing from home for several months and the letters made glad our hearts, but at the same time brought sorrow to some of us.

Advance on Vicksburg

The last few days of June were marked by unusual activity of staff officers, orders to keep rations cooked, ready to move at a moment's warning and other signs, all portended an early advance. On June 29th, the expected orders were issued and we took up the line of march, camping the first night at Beatty's Bluff. The next morning by daylight we were on the road headed towards Vicksburg, which all of us believed to be our destination, and a hard half day's march brought us to Vernon where we remained the afternoon and night.

July 1st and 2nd we had exceedingly irregular and tiresome marching: roads blocked by wagons and artillery; dry, hot and dusty we were continually on our feet, but made little progress. Orders issued to allow no music from bands, beating of drums nor any noise above ordinary tone of conversation. Late in the afternoon we halted, faced front and moved a few steps out of the road and camped in the line just as we had been marching. We remained in that position through the night and all day of the third wondering why delays were so frequent and of such long duration. Our idea of generalship was that if our expedition was intended for the relief of Vicksburg, it should be a bold and quick movement. It was irritating to be dallying along at the rate we were going, but we had implicit confidence in General Johnston and hoped all would turn out well.

The memorable Fourth of July found us awaiting orders to advance, which never came, and an ominous silence prevailed in the region about Vicksburg, to whose guns we had been listening the past three months. "What does it mean?" was the question on every tongue, but we could only conjecture and no one who possessed the information would impart it to us. We lay there in suspense all of the 4th and 5th, orders prohibiting all noise strictly enforced, not a drum to be heard nor a bugle note, everything "still as death". A funeral would not have been more somber.

At one a.m. on the 6th, we were aroused from our slumbers and officially informed that Vicksburg had surrendered. "Surrendered on the Fourth of July." We immediately "fell in" and, taking the back track, marched about a mile when we had to give the road for the wagons and artillery to pass to the front; then with solemn tread and downcast hearts began another retreat towards Jackson. The day was one of the hottest of the summer, the dust stirred by the train of wagons was stifling, no water on the route, many fell by the wayside exhausted. Our canteens were drained before half the morning passed and not another drop of water did we see until 2:00 p.m. We came to a pond in an open field into which 300 thirsty beef cattle had plunged, stirring the slimy mud from the bottom until it was thick as gruel and so hot it almost blistered the throat when swallowed. But we were compelled to drink the filthy stuff and, as bad as it was, it saved the lives of many of the men.

Although not pressed by the enemy, we lost no time, having just enough skirmishing in the rear to keep stragglers well closed up. A two day march brought us to camps on the bank of Pearl River at 6:00 p.m. on the seventh.

Siege of Jackson

The 8th of July opened with heavy skirmishing and cannonading in front, our cavalry being gradually driven back, but we remained quietly in camps getting a good day's rest. At daylight on the 9th we formed line of battle in shape of a semicircle, the right resting on Pearl River above, and left on the river below the city. The order of formation by divisions from right to left, Loring, French, Walker, Breckenridge, our brigade (Buford's) being on the extreme right, but towards noon we were moved back and held in reserve at the Governor's Mansion. Our cavalry having been driven in, during the night the enemy established their lines parallel with ours and, as near as they could approach without coming within range of the guns of the infantry, began fortifying for itself and when completed we faced north by companies, but could immediately resume our position in line when necessary. General Johnston passing down the line noticed our traverses and asked why we had so many ditches. "Just wait till the next bomb shell comes along and you will see why." The answer was barely finished when a shell came shrieking just over our heads and the General replied, "The explanation is satisfactory" and rode off laughing. One of the enemy's guns had the exact range of our regiment and fired regularly every five minutes for forty-eight hours, but it was an easy matter to dodge a shell for each company kept a man on the breastworks to watch for the smoke in daylight and the flash at night. When the gun fired he would yell "look out" and we had time to jump in the ditch before the shell reached us. It was a waste of ammunition so far as the damage to us was concerned for during the forty-eight hours constant firing we did not have a man hurt by it.

From July 9th to 16th, cannonading and picket fighting were incessant day and night and occasional assaults were made on some parts of our lines all of which were repulsed, usually with severe loss to the enemy. The 27th Alabama

39

was not engaged in anything that might be ranked as a battle, our fighting being confined to the skirmish lines where we took it by turns and sometimes they made it so hot for us that it very much resembled a real battle.

On the 14th a truce was agreed upon for the purpose of burying the dead. The bang of small arms and thunder of cannon ceased, perfect quiet reigned, a pleasant respite from the exciting times of the five days preceding. Many of us met the boys in blue on "halfway" ground and held friendly conversation with them while the gruesome work was carried on. At 4:00 p.m. the tap of the drum warned us that "recess" was over, and we hastened back to the cover of our ditches.

Another Retreat

In the afternoon of July 16th, teams were geared up, ammunition removed, and all signs indicated an evacuation. At dark the artillery silently withdrew from position and passed through the town in the direction of the river and at 10 o'clock the infantry began moving, leaving only the picket line to entertain the enemy. All was exceedingly quiet except the "bang" of the pickets, which extended all around the line and was more constant and vigorous than at any time during the siege. By 2 a.m. of the 17th the last of the troops, except the pickets, had safely crossed the river and we felt very much relieved. The darkness of the night, the deep sand in the road and the blockade of the wagons and artillery rendered the march extremely slow and tiresome.

Weary and sleepy we trudged along all night and the following day until 4 p.m. when we halted and spread our blankets on the roadside in good condition to enjoy an all night's sleep. We expected a vigorous pursuit by the enemy's overwhelming force, but in this we were agreeably disappointed. They seemed to have no disposition to follow and after the first day we moved leisurely, stopping when and where our commanders saw fit.

Being in no condition to inaugurate an offensive movement it was not necessary to have so many idle troops which were needed in other departments. Some were sent to reinforce General Bragg, others to Mobile, until only Loring's division was left and we spent the entire summer and early fall very quietly on the lines of railroad between Jackson and Meridian, at Morton, Newton, Forest and other stations.

Rations were reasonable plentiful and on July 28th we drew six months pay which enabled us to buy vegetables and occasionally a chicken or a dozen eggs, so we lived sumptuously as long as our money lasted. The buying capacity of our money was somewhat limited as chickens cost $2.00 to $3.00 each, eggs $1.50 per dozen, melons $5.00 to $10.00 and other things in proportion. Some of the boys did not depend altogether on buying, crops were fine, roasting ears and sweet potatoes "ripe" and frequent raids were made on the neighboring corn fields and potato patches. Almost every morning piles of corn and sacks of potatoes could be seen in camps. How they got there no one seemed to know but, being of a perishable nature, it would be too bad to let them go to waste and they were consumed without any conscientious scruples so far as I ever knew. In consequence of these depredations, very strict orders were issued to call the roll five times a day and if anyone was absent without leave, the regiment had to be marched to General Buford's headquarters and drilled till next roll call, the severest punishment was to be meted out to anyone guilty of stealing. These orders were enforced for a few days then gradually relaxed until we were allowed about as much liberty as we could reasonably expect. Passes were issued freely and one or more from each mess would often go foraging and bring in good things to eat.

On one occasion, Company C failed to get the usual supply and this is how it happened. Ike Landers and George Pool stole out by the guards on a dark night, each with a sack under his arm, and about a mile from camp, accidently or otherwise, took a near cut through a potato patch. The owner had been losing potatoes for some time and that particular night was hid behind a stump, with a double-barrel shotgun, watching for the thieves. The boys happened to discover him before they began digging and very unceremoniously "lit out" in the opposite direction. The old gentleman waited until they ran 30 or 40 yards and then pulled down on them with both barrels. Ike brought away a portion of the old man's bird shot, but George escaped unharmed though badly scared. George said, "me be dad rot if he didn't clear a stake and rider a fence and never tach a rail." The next morning Ike complained of his back being very sore and, going into the woods with him, we stripped off his shirt and sure enough his back looked like he had a good case of chicken pox. The shot were small and, as the old man had considerately waited to shoot at long range, they were only skin deep, so we did not think the case of sufficient gravity to call in a surgeon. We picked the shot out with a sharp pointed knife blade and the officers were never the wiser.

Furloughs and Salvation

On July 25th orders from the War Department were read on dress parade to furlough one man out of every 25, and all except two officers to each company. It was decided to give the Camp Douglas prisoners the preference and an exciting contest was inaugurated to determine who should be the lucky ones, the rest of us having to content ourselves with writing letters to send by the men. This we considered a great privilege as it was so seldom we had an opportunity to send letters. All the pencils in the regiment were busy the next few hours writing to homefolk, sweethearts and friends. Many of us who lived on the north side of the Tennessee River had but little hope of our letters reaching their destination as the enemy occupied all that part of the state. We expected the boys to be captured but they succeeded in getting through the lines and eluded the Yankees by lying in thickets a large part of the time they were home.

About the 1st of August our chaplain, Coffee, assisted by Reverend Dr. Burns and Lt. Davis, of the 12th Louisiana, began a revival meeting in camp which grew to large proportions and continued through the summer. As before stated, we were in the piney woods and fat pine knots were scattered in profusion all over the woods. We gathered these into piles and, when ignited, they illuminated the meeting grounds which was attended by large numbers every night. Hundreds of penitents gathered around the altar and many were converted. A Christian Association was organized embracing all denominations and before the meetings closed large accessions were made to it. This association was continued through the war and no doubt thousands of Confederate soldiers owe their salvation to the influences brought to bear upon them during their service in the army.

In Camps

Two or three weeks was about as long as we were allowed to remain at any one place. They kept us moving partly to vary the monotony of camp life, but more particularly to keep us in training for the march when it should become necessary. Sometimes we longed for something more exciting than lying around in the woods fifty or a hundred miles from the enemy, but usually we were cheerful and enjoyed the good easy time we were having. Soldiers would have fun whether in camp, on the march, or even on the battle field. Always something to laugh at and talk about, and no doubt that disposition had the happy effect of keeping up the health and spirits of an army.

We had a good deal of sickness while roaming around in Big Black swamp, but a change to "piney" woods restored us to excellent health, and blessed with good appetites we were able to consume much more than our regular daily rations. No enemy being near, we had no picketing to do, no digging ditches, and but little drilling. This left us with plenty of time to indulge in fun and games, one of the favorite pastimes being playing cards for melons. One would buy or "hook" a melon and ten or a dozen put up one dollar each and played "seven up" for it. The winner putting it up again and so on until tired of the game, then dividing it into as many slices as players and all eat it. We did not consider this gambling as the money was not the object, but staked merely to add interest to the game.

That the reader may have a little insight into the manner of spending the time when not engaged in active operations against the enemy, I will quote from my diary just a few reminiscences of the summer campaign.

Diary Entry, August 13, 14 & 15:

The past three days have been spent in clearing up camps, frolicking, and having lots of fun. One incident particularly afforded us a good deal of amusement, and as I have nothing else to record in my diary, and no duty to perform, I will try to write it up. I know I cannot describe it half as funny as it occurred.

Jess Clanton, scissors in hand, took a seat on a log and drawled out, "Boys, I want my ha'r cut."

No one spoke, and after a short pause, "Boys, don't all speak at once; some o' you fellers come here and cut my ha'r."

Another and longer pause, and Nat Pool said, "Jess, it seems like no one will volunteer; I reckon I'll have to cut your hair, but I don't like to do it a bit."

"Nat, can you cut ha'r?"

"Why, Jess, I'm the best barber you ever saw; I'm a barber from Barbertown, I tell you."

"When did you ever cut any ha'r?"

"I used to cut all the boys' hair before the war. They come for miles around, and I had a regular hair-cutting every Saturday."

"Well, why ain't you said so before?"

"Oh, I don't want to be bothered by you fellows, which I knew would be the case if you found out what a good barber I am."

"Nat, I don't believe you can cut ha'r, but I'm goin' to let you try it anyhow."

Nat took the scissors, and starting at the back of his neck made a clean path over the top to the forehead, then beginning behind the left ear went diagonally over to the right temple, likewise from right ear to left temple, a few circular turns around the base of the cranium and some patches off the top, and closing the scissors said, "Jess, I'm done."

Jess surveyed his tattered locks in a three-cornered piece of looking-glass, laid it down and very coolly remarked, "Nat, I'm goin' to whup you."

"What for Jess?"

"For spilin' by ha'r, that's what fur!"

"Why Jess that's the latest style; if you'll notice, all the Generals and Colonels have their hair cut that way."

"I don't care nothin' about the Ginerals, nor Kurnels, I'm goin' to whup you."

"Jess, you can't do it."

"Yes I can and I'll show you how quick I can do it."

"Dry up, Jess; you know I can wear you out before you can say Jack Robinson."

The boys gathered around as they always do when there is a chance for fun or a fight. Nat is a great practical joker, always having fun at the expense of others, and has a peculiar knack of coming out best; but we were determined he should not bluff nor joke Jess out of it this time and began to encourage him. "Stand up to him Jess; we'll see you through."

Jess got more aggressive and Nat more serious; he tried his jokes and "bluffs" in vain. By this time the whole regiment and some from other regiments had gathered around in a solid mass. Bill Summerhill popped his heels together. "Jump up little nigger and jar de groun'! Stan' up to him Jess; I'm at your back."

Finally Jess says, "Nat, I'll let you off on one condition."

"What's that?"

"You'll set right thar on that log and let me cut your ha'r."

"I'll never do it."

"But you will; I'm going to have ha'r or blud."

Matters were beginning to look squally for Nat. He wouldn't fight, and didn't want to have his hair cut, and couldn't run for the dense crowd which encircled them, and all hallooing of Jess.

Rolling up his sleeves, "Give us more room boys; I'm goin' for him now," he started towards Nat.

"Hold on, hold on, Jess; let's talk this matter over in a friendly way."

"Nothin' but ha'r or blud. No time for talkin'. I'm goin' to wear the very innards ouwen you, and that mightily quick, if you don't set right down thar and let me cut yer ha'r."

It was too much for Nat; everybody was against him, and there was no alternative but to fight or have his hair cut. He prized his black, shiny locks very highly, but rather than risk a fisticuff encounter with Jess, he reluctantly yielded and said, "If nothing else will satisfy you, Jess, I reckon I'll have to let you cut it; but if I stay in the army 10 years these dad-blamed fellows will never let me hear the last of it."

Handing him the scissors, Nat took his seat on the same log and Jess proceeded to do up his head in about the same style as his own. When he had completed the job he called for the looking-glass and said, "Now, Nat, look at yourself; you look jest like a Gineral."

"Yes, I reckon I do look like a "Gineral", but it's a gineral durned fool."

This is the first time we have ever seen Nat "beaten at his own game." He is completely crest-fallen, and, as he said, it will be a long time before he hears the last of it.

Inspection of Camps

One morning Colonel Jackson walked through camps and, as if the thought had just then occurred to him, remarked, "Boys, I was notified this morning that General Buford would come around this morning at 10 o'clock inspecting camps. I am glad to see you haven't any cobs and shucks in your camp." He then returned to headquarters and as soon as he was out of sight we set to work gathering them up and in a very short space of time had a wagon load of cobs and shucks carried to the woods and covered with leaves. We then cut "brush brooms" and swept the streets between companies, adjusted our gun stacks, arranged accoutrements and had everything in nice order for inspection.

Promptly at the appointed time the General and Colonel Jackson, followed by their staff, rode through, scanning everything closely. At the end of the line they turned and rode back, stopping about the middle of the regiment. We gathered around expecting a compliment on the tidy appearance of our camp, but were sadly disappointed. The staff officers were smiling, but the General wore a frown on his face, and he could look extremely ferocious when things didn't suit him. After a short silence, he said, "Jackson, this beats the d——."

"Why? What's the matter, General?"

"The 27th Alabama is the only regiment in the brigade that eats corn cob and shuck without leaving any sign."

We expected further investigation and were a little fearful of the result, but I suppose the General concluded he was beaten and they rode off to the next regiment, which was the 9th Arkansas. The "signs" were abundant over there, the ground almost covered with shucks and cobs. The General ordered the Colonel to form the regiment and march them to his headquarters. He then had the Colonel to drill them under his supervision until they could hardly stand.

Buying a "Coverlid"

When September came in, the days were about as hot as August had been, but the nights were getting cool and we felt the need of more covering. The Government was unable to furnish us blankets and those we brought from home were so thin from long, continuous use that they afforded but little protection from the cold. We often had to get up the latter part of the night to replenish the fires to keep at all comfortable.

We bunked three together in order to economize bedding, stretching one blanket to ward off rain and heavy dew. The writer and his two bunk-mates had been reduced to two blankets, so when we had one stretched over us, it left only one for both bed and cover, and we were determined to have more if it was to be found in that part of Mississippi. We did not expect to get a blanket, as the Confederacy had already been stripped of everything of that class for the use of soldiers. We thought we might induce some old lady to part with a quilt, which would answer the purpose. Procuring a pass we started on the search and visited several farm houses where we were told they had given up everything to the soldiers and had nothing to spare. However discouraged, we kept going from house to house until we found an old lady who said she had a "coverlid" which she would sell if she could get her price, "Well, how much do you ask for it, Mrs.?" She replied, "Forty dollars." We were not burdened with Confederate money and it behooved us to drive as good a bargain as possible, so we concluded to resort to a little "Jewing" and replied, "Oh, that is too much, we can't give any such price." To which the Mrs. countered, "I reckon I o'r't to know what it's worth. I spun every bit of the thread and wove it all by myself. The 'fillin' in that coverlid is all wool, and it's worth $40.00 if it's worth a cent."

"But just think of it, we get only $11.00 a month and at that price it would take near four months to pay for it."

"It's not my fault they don't give you but $11.00 a month."

"But you've used it 20 years and ought to sell it cheap to soldiers."

"I don't care if I have used it 20 years, I've took good care of it, and if you don't give $40.00, you don't get it."

The parleying continued for quite a while, and when we saw the old lady begin to weaken a little, we presented three new $10 Confederate bills and the temptation was too great. She took the bills and handed us the "coverlid". It was a good one too, almost as large as a small tent fly and it did good service for us all the winter.

March to Canton

We received orders several times during September to move and it was generally believed we would to General Bragg's army, but as often orders were countermanded. When positive orders did come, it happened probably on the most unpropitious day of the year. It was the last day of the month and had been raining hard all day. At 10 o'clock we were notified to cook all the rations on hand and be ready to march at 4:00 p.m.

The rain increased in severity, drowned out our fires, and flooded the camps. Our rations, cooked and uncooked, were soaked with water, such another "mess" was hardly ever seen. At 5:00 p.m. it seemed as if the flood gates of heaven were all opened, but in the midst of it we formed line, and moved out. When night came there was no abatement of the rain and the darkness was so impenetrable we might as well have been blindfolded. Colonel Jackson rode a white horse which was somewhat of a guide for the foremost man, and the rest of us could follow only by the noise in front of us, some singing merrily while others were laughing at the unfortunate comrades who were constantly falling into mud holes and ditches. If any one of the regiment escaped falling he was lucky indeed. Often one would fall and half a dozen or more would stumble over him, until they were piled three or four deep.

Near midnight, we stopped alongside a large farm and soon had a rousing fire made of the farmer's rails. The rain ceased about this time and, having scraped off the mud and wrung out our clothes the best we could, we settled down before the fires for rest and sleep. We were in motion the next morning by day break and a hard day's march brought us to Pearl River at sunset. Here we learned that Canton was our destination, to reinforce Jackson's cavalry, who were fighting near that town.

Having but one small boat which carried half a regiment at a trip, we made slow progress crossing the river, but after so long a time all got across and arrived near Canton at 4:00 p.m., October 2nd going into the same camps we had left four months previously.

The enemy had retired to Big Black before our arrival and we had nothing to do but fix up camps and make ourselves as comfortable as possible. It seemed almost like being at home and we were well pleased with the surroundings with one exception. That was the miserable water we had to get for drinking and all other purposes, from mud holes and ponds. We pulled crab-grass which was abundant in the fields and, having placed poles in the shape of a tent, covered them with the grass, which made comfortable houses that were rain proof and warm; we made beds of the same material.

Then followed a series of drills, reviews, and big meetings, which were resumed as soon as we had got settled. These duties occupied our time till October 15th, when report came that a large force was moving on Grenada a hundred miles north of us. We were ordered to reinforce General Chalmers there. We cooked rations all night and the next morning double-quicked three miles to Canton, boarded a freight train arriving at Grenada at 2:00 p.m. and found the enemy had arrived also. After several days fighting with General Chalmers, we received a telegram on October 17th to hurry back to Canton. The Yankees were advancing in large force and we immediately started on the return trip. All went well until 9 o'clock that night when a terrific storm of wind and rain set in. Those on top were almost blown from their moorings and begged for standing room inside, but every foot of space was occupied and they were jokingly told to "never mind the weather so the wind don't blow, that's the way to get your independence boys,", etc. They were mad enough to have charged us with bayonets, but they couldn't get to us while the train was in motion. By the time the storm had subsided they had cooled off in a good humor. Thirty miles from Canton we were ordered to load and be wide awake as the enemy were expected to make a dash on the train, but we were not interrupted and reached Canton at 3:00 a.m. At daylight we marched out to meet the enemy who sure enough were advancing from Clinton and had gone but a few miles when our cavalry, which preceded us, struck the front of the column and a brisk fight ensued.

We immediately formed our line, deployed skirmishers and raising the "Rebel yell", rushed forward. But before we could fire a gun they wheeled and made tracks in the direction from which they had come. It proved to be only a large raiding party of cavalry and, as we could not pursue on foot, we remained in position while General Jackson's cavalry pressed them and continued the pursuit as evidenced by the receding boom of the guns until nightfall.

The next day we returned to our same camps and were surprised to find all our grass houses had mysteriously disappeared, swept away as clean as if a cyclone had struck them. The mystery was explained when we learned the farmers had hauled them away and had them snugly stored in their barns for winter feed. To say that we were provoked is putting it mildly and some of the boys even went so far as to use language which would not look well in print, but it was an established fact that they were gone. Not knowing how soon we might be called away again, we did not rebuild at once, but lay around under the trees for some days, when the cutting November winds and cold rains admonished us that it would be wise to provide for the worst weather which might be expected later. This time we resolved to build of more substantial material than grass.

Building Winter Quarters

Procuring all the axes in the regiment and borrowing saws and frows from the neighboring farmers, we set to work cutting timber and riving boards. All this had to be done between drills, reviews and other duties, and required considerable time and labor. We put in all our spare time and before November was gone we had substantial log houses covered with boards, cracks chinked and daubed, stick and dirt chimneys and could sit by our own firesides, bidding defiance to the elements—provided the Yankees would be good and let us enjoy the fruit of our labor. We lived in constant dread that the enemy would make some move, or something else happen to draw us out of our good camp, and if we could have had assurance in the beginning that we were permanently located for four months, our contentment would have been as near perfect as 'twas possible to be.

One pound of meal, one pound of beef, with an occasional slice of bacon was our daily ration. This was very good as far as it went, but not as much as a healthy soldier could eat especially when, as was often the case, the meat was half bone. However, the paymaster had been more punctual than usual during the summer and fall and we were able to indulge in "luxuries" such as cabbage, stock peas, and potatoes which we bought from citizens. Sweet potatoes were abundant and cheaper than anything else. They were the largest, sweetest and best we had ever seen and supplied a large part of our living, but got to be so common they were not prized as highly as other food. We had lots of fun stealing them from each other. When a fellow put one in the fire to roast he had to watch it constantly or he would never get so much as a taste of it.

As soon as we got settled down in camps our chaplain, Coffee, assisted by his co-workers, Lt. Davis and Dr. Burns, revived the big meeting. Brother Coffee was a zealous laborer in the Lord's vineyard and certainly had a field where the harvest was ripe for the exercise of his zeal. We made seats of split logs and erected a stand for him in a beautiful grove where he held services day and night, when other duties were not pressing us too much. The ladies of Canton and vicinity often attended services, the older ones taking an active part in the work at the altar, while the younger set were merely interested spectators. There was also a younger set of the boys who were not so much concerned about their soul's salvation, as they were of the charms of the young ladies, and many a pleasant hour passed only too quickly. The revival continued through the winter resulting in the conversion of great numbers and large additions to the roll of the Christian Association.

While a large portion of the 27th and other regiments attended the services punctually, many others who were not concerned about their spiritual welfare, engaged in sports of different character. Games, such as seven-up, chuck-a-luck, and poker were very common, but the diversion which was most universally indulged in was the old school boy game of "town ball". All except the older men of the regiment played with the zest of school boys, some of the officers taking part while others, including General Buford, were interested spectators. Horse racing also was a frequent amusement. We had a nice level track of 600 yards along side our camps which the officers used for exercise of their horses. On one occasion all the horses of the 27th and 25th Alabama were brought out and a purse of $100.00 was quickly made up for the fastest horse. Both regiments turned out en masse and we had an exciting time the next two hours.

When the races were over, the winner sent the money to town and invested all of it in whiskey, which was set out free to everybody. Many of the boys accepted the initiation with little persuasion and as a result only a short time elapsed before officers and men were in a glorious state of intoxication, yelling like savages and acting lunatics generally. All passed off in fun until a large squad made a dash on the sutler's tent and cleaned it out before the astonished Dutchman could comprehend what had happened. The guards were called out and arrested the rioters but too late to save any of the sutler's stock. It nearly broke the poor fellow's heart to see all his wealth wiped out at one swoop. This was the first and last sutler's stock we ever had in the regiment.

Some may say the recital of such incidents had better be suppressed, but the history of the regiment would not be complete without narrating some of the bad as well as the good. Besides, it was generally conceded that soldiers might properly indulge in practises in war times, which would be inexcusable at home in times of peace. The inclination to indulge in intoxicating beverages might have existed with a great many but it was only at long intervals that such opportunities occurred and when they did occur they were often carried to extremes.

We had a splendid drill ground and our education in that line was not neglected, as we drilled more during our stay here than in all our two years service. General Buford instituted competitive drills between the different regiments of his brigade, which aroused such a spirit of emulation that we became very proficient in Hardee's tactics. As in our religious meetings the ladies attended our drills and reviews, which added to the interest of the exercises and their presence inspired companies and regiments with the desire to excel. We really enjoyed the brigade reviews which were held near camps, but the division reviews being seven miles away were not so pleasant. General Polk took command of the army of Mississippi in January and, of course, on his first visit to us had to review the division. Accompanied by General Forrest and Governor Harris of Tennessee, he marched us out to the grounds where we were on parade for two or three hours without dinner, and made the return trip consuming the entire day. We were well nigh exhausted when we got back to camps after night and no supper cooked.

The first half of January was said to be the coldest weather experienced in that region for years, but we were so well prepared for it with our comfortable houses and plenty of firewood, there was no suffering from cold, although the majority of the regiment was sadly in need of clothing, blankets, and shoes. We drew clothing only one time during the winter, three jackets, three shorts, six pair of drawers, two pair of pants, two pair socks to the company. No shoes nor blankets which were needed worst of all. Two companies received a consignment from home, which supplied them fairly well, but taking all into consideration, we had no cause to grumble and sympathy was often expressed for our comrades whose lots were cast in the colder climates of Virginia and Tennessee.

Fun and frolic enlivened the time when not engaged in soldierly duties, and all we had to mar our pleasures was the certainty that with the breaking up of bad weather we would have to enter upon a campaign of marching, fighting and other hardships.

In the latter part of the month the cold subsided, the sun shone bright and spring like, the occasional rumble of guns in the distance, the galloping of couriers to and from headquarters, indicated that our good times were fast drawing to a close. On the night of January 31, 1864 a very interesting prayer meeting was rudely broken up by the announcement from the stand of orders to prepare to move at once. A very sudden transition from prayers of Christians, groans of penitents, to confusion and bustle was perceivable. Three days rations were issued and, having such a scarcity of cooking vessels, it took the greater part of the night to get our "grub" ready for the haversack, but when morning came we had no further orders about moving. The next few days we were lying around camps with baggage all packed, receiving orders one hour which were countermanded the next, a state of uncertainty and suspense prevailing among officers as well as men. We continued jerking all the beef we could get and judging from the piles of hard cornbread and black sooty beef one might have thought we expected to stand the siege. The firing approached nearer day by day, but seemed to be bearing towards Jackson and it was evident the enemy were driving our cavalry, and that city was their objective point. Couriers brought the information that Sherman was moving with 40,000–50,000 men, while we had only our division of 5000 or 6000 to oppose him.

On the night of January 4, positive orders were read commanding us to be ready to move by daylight, accordingly we were in line at the appointed time, wagons and baggage started to the rear. Col. Jackson proposed three cheers for the best camp we ever had, which were given with heartfelt earnestness. We moved out on the Jackson road and kept up a brisk pace all the forenoon, meeting excited couriers at short intervals who reported overwhelming numbers of the enemy. Having covered 13 miles, we were about to come in contact with one of the columns and were quickly thrown into line of battle, not with the expectation of making an attack, for our force was too weak to risk a battle. While maneuvering, additional information was received that another large column had already occupied Jackson. This placed us in a predicament that required prompt action, as we were liable to be cut off and captured, so changing our course we crossed Pearl River and made a rapid march the next two days to place ourselves in front of the enemy.

We camped the third night on the same ground we had left that dark, rainy night four months before, and the next morning, reinforced by General French's division, moved back towards Jackson to learn something more of the movements and intentions of the enemy. Six miles from our starting point we met them in such large force that after some skirmishing we were forced to fall back to Morton, where we established our line and skirmishing continued till night put an end to it.

The radical change from a life of "ease and luxury" such as we enjoyed all winter to a campaign of marching, fighting, sleeping out in winter weather with scanty clothing and blankets was pretty severe. Our feet were already blistered, muscles so sore, and joints so stiff we were in poor condition for a fight or a retreat. The latter expedient seeming to be the more probable, which proved to be the case, but a little later when pressed by the Bluecoats, we were able to make a fair record as sprinters, regardless of blisters and stiffened joints.

After the skirmishing ceased we hoped to get a night's rest and were ordered to sleep on arms, but as soon as it was dark enough to cover our movements, the wagons and artillery started and by 10 o'clock we were in full retreat, our brigade being the rear guard. We now had about 10,000 men, but were so largely outnumbered that Sherman could place an equal number in our front and still have twice as many more to operate on our flanks. We marched all night, all the next day and till 11:00 p.m. when we had to cook rations before getting any sleep, having been on foot 40 hours and were almost completely exhausted.

Briefly told, the retreat from Morton to Meridian was only a repetition of the last two days experience, skirmishing by day and retreating at night, snatching a little sleep when the opportunity offered, all we were able to do was to harass and delay the enemy. February 11th, we established a line of battle on Chunky Mountain, with orders to hold our position at all hazards. Skirmishing was very brisk all day, but they seemed to have no disposition to come to close quarters and we could not afford to force the fighting, so darkness ended the conflict with but few casualties on either side. In a very few minutes after the firing ceased, all except the pickets were sound asleep, but we didn't get to enjoy it long. At 10 o'clock we were aroused and orders whispered to move out silently, following file leaders, as no commands would be spoken. Half asleep, we stole away in the darkness and a dreary and tiresome tramp all night brought us to Meridian.

Here we formed another line for the purpose of delaying the enemy while the remaining government stores were removed. Light skirmishing and picket fighting kept us employed all day and at night we extended our line as far as it could be stretched, gathered pine knots in stacks as high as a man's head. When they got to burning a brilliant array of lights illuminated the country over a space long enough for an army of 20,000 men. We thought we would make Sherman believe we had large reinforcements, but didn't fool him much. He kept his flanking columns moving to our rear, and at 1 o'clock we drew off and began another night retreat.

The next three days and nights we were closely pressed and forced to form successive lines of battle. Brisk skirmishing, which sometimes almost rose to the dignity of a battle continued to the height of February 16th when we crossed the Tombigbee River and the pursuit was abandoned. On our retreat out of Mississippi, the people flocked to the roadside to "see the soldiers" and expressed much astonishment to see such a big army running from the Yankees. They had never seen an army before and imagined our 10,000 men enough to whip all the Yankees in Mississippi, but no doubt they were still more amazed when they saw Sherman's 50,000 Bluecoats following like blood hounds on our trail.

After we crossed the Tombigbee River we had no Yankees acting as rear guard to keep us closed up, no forming line of battle to check the enemy, then double-quicking to overtake the command. Discipline was not enforced so strictly as to keep us in our proper places in line. The roads being muddy and in bad condition we were allowed to select the firm ground on the roadside avoiding mud hoes and bad places, so we had an easy time, going into camp that night near Demopolis. Once more in camp on the soil of our native state we hoped to remain long enough for our blistered feet to heal and to recover from the arduous campaign of thirteen days and nights' constant retreating and skirmishing.

On February 22, 1864 large reinforcements began to arrive from the army of Tennessee. Every train was loaded and we were ordered to have three days cooked rations on hand ready to march at a moment's notice. We expected to move back as soon as we could collect an army sufficient to justify forward movement. We anticipated great pleasure in chasing Sherman back to Vicksburg, but on the 24th we learned that after destroying the railroad and what stores we left in Meridian, he was falling back to Jackson. Our reinforcements were then returned to the army of Tennessee at Dalton, leaving only Loring's division and Ector's brigade in the vicinity of Demopolis.

Our program being entirely changed by Sherman's retrograde movement, it seemed probable there would be no active operations in our department for some time. Colonel Jackson of the 27th and Colonel Ives of the 35th Alabama got up a petition asking leave to carry their regiments to North Alabama for the purpose of recruiting. At first, General Buford was averse to the proposed expedition but reluctantly yielded and endorsed the application. Although our losses had been light, considering the length of time we had been in service, deaths in prison and from disease, and quite a number still in prison at that time had reduced the number of effective men in the two regiments to about 200 men each. Of course we were very anxious to go but had little hope, although General Polk had expressed a great desire to recruit his army in some way. While waiting in suspense what the result of our application was we had a very quiet time and resumed our regular camp duties, enjoying the rest and recuperating our vigor for whatever might turn up.

On the first day of March it was announced that money was on hand to pay us up to date, but it was the old issue of Confederate which was much depreciated. If we would wait awhile the new issue would be worth 33 percent more. Some favored waiting, but others argued that "a bird in hand is worth two in the bush," besides the new issue might never be issued and after considerable discussion it was decided to settle the matter by election. Preliminaries were arranged, judges appointed, and the voting commenced lively, a more exciting election was rarely ever held. When the votes were counted it was found the old issue had won by a large majority and when it was distributed—wages, bounty and commutation—we had our pockets bulging with money, about $200 to each man. Then to fill our cup of happiness to the brim, we received orders to cook two days rations and be ready to march to North Alabama early the next morning. Such glorious news we couldn't sleep, but sat around the camp fires planning and talking about the enjoyment we would have at home, until late in the night. A large majority of the regiment had not been home since enlistment in December 1861 and had no communication with home folks except at long intervals.

March 4th, 1864 at 8 a.m. the order to fall in was obeyed with unusual alacrity, and the 27th and 35th Alabama moved out with quick step and light hearts. A tramp of 200 miles was before us, or those of us who lived north of the Tennessee River, but that was only a trifle when our faces were set homeward. Marching by General Buford's headquarters we gave him three cheers and while the 12th Louisiana band played "Home, Sweet Home" we proudly kept time with the strains.

We made 16 to 25 miles a day and there was less complaint of fatigue perhaps than on any march we ever made. The fertile country through which we passed had never been overrun by the army and was indeed a land of plenty. We fared sumptuously until we struck the Sand Mountains. The citizens along the route seemed to take great pleasure in contributing to our comfort in every possible way, especially at the beautiful little town of Eutaw, where we stopped for an hour rest. The whole town turned out, men, women and children with baskets of provisions and fed the four hundred, leaving fragments which we gathered up and carried away in our haversacks. We spent the greater portion of one day at Tuscaloosa, where we found business going on as if it wasn't "wartime", though the stocks were much depleted. Having plenty of money, we could not resist the temptation of sprucing up a little, being desirous of appearing as neat as possible when we reached home, though every purchase we made cut deep into our pocket books. As a sample of the prices we paid, the writer selected a boy's work hat (worth about 50 cents now) and asked the price, "$75.00." "You certainly don't mean $75.00 for that little wool hat?", I exclaimed. The proprietor replied, "I most certainly do; so far as I know these are all the hats in Alabama, and when they are gone, I can't get any more". I bought the hat and some other necessary articles at corresponding prices and my pocket book was reduced to a skeleton in a very short space of time. The two regiments had just drawn about $80,000 and, at a reasonable estimate, they must have left one-third of it in Tuscaloosa that day.

After leaving Tuscaloosa, we soon struck the Sand Mountains, where nearly all the people sympathized with the enemy and bushwhackers were numerous. Ever ready to pounce upon a lone rebel who might chance to stray away from his command, we kept close to the main body. When we entered Franklin County, the homes of Companies B and G, they were furloughed and left us.

On March 11th we met many citizens and straggling soldiers hurrying south as fast as horses, mules, and vehicles could carry them. They were badly demoralized, and reported the Tennessee valley full of Yankees. However, we continued on hoping it was but a small force and we would be able to drive them back. About the middle of the day a courier from Colonel Moreland brought the information that 12,000 Yankees were, sure enough, in the valley and all our cavalry were retreating to Columbus. A consultation of our officers resulted in a decision to fall back, await further developments and send to Columbus for subsistence which could not be procured in that section. Consequently, a march of 25 miles brought us back to the same camps we had left early in the morning. We spent the next day in camps and our force was augmented by a large party of refugees among whom were some nice young ladies, and we young fellows enjoyed the day so much we would have been content to remain there indefinitely.

That night we received the cheering news that the enemy had retired to Decatur, and on the following morning, with renewed hope, we resumed the march. On the third day we reached a point where we could overlook the beautiful valley of the Tennessee and some of us imagined we could almost locate the spot where our homes lay beyond the winding river. Descending the mountain we pitched our camp at Mt. Hope, but before we had time to get well rested for our long tramp, a large raiding force came out from Decatur and we retreated down the valley of Russellville.

On March 18th all who lived South of the river were furloughed, leaving Companies C, E and I from Lauderdale and Company I from Madison of the 27th and one or two companies of the 35th, in all about 125 men. We rejoiced with the favored ones, but almost wept that we were so "near home, yet so far."

On March 20th, a report reached us that Federal Cavalry were operating in the vicinity of Moulton impressing provisions, driving off cattle, etc. Colonel Jackson proposed that we make an investigation and if not too many for us we would give them a good "thrashing" and send them back to Decatur. Accordingly, we took an early start the next morning in the direction of Moulton and had proceeded unmolested till ten o'clock when all of a sudden we were greeted with a volley from a concealed foe, the bullets whistling all about us. Colonel Jackson gave the command, "Fix bayonets, forward, double quick." With the rebel yell we went at them, but they would not wait for a closer acquaintance, and as they galloped over a hill in plain view we estimated that there were about 75 in the company. They made several stands before reaching Moulton, retiring each time when we got near enough for our Enfield rifles to reach them.

At Moulton we were joined by a squad of Confederate Cavalry, eight or ten in number who were scouting in the vicinity and were attracted by the firing. We placed them in front and found them very useful in locating the enemy when they made a stand, skirmishing with them till we came up. Two miles beyond Moulton they made stubborn stand, having the advantage of a hill with open space in front. We preferred to dislodge them without exposing ourselves in the field if possible, but the range being too long for our rifles, we had to resort to the charge in which John D. Williams of Lauderdale County was killed, the only casualty we suffered during the day.

We followed on driving them almost to Decatur, when night overtook us and we had to abandon the chase. We then retraced our steps arriving at Moulton at ten o'clock, weary and hungry. Having been on foot 16 hours, without taking time to stack our guns, we threw everything on the ground, rolled up in blankets and were soon fast asleep.*

If anyone had predicted a ten inch snow in that climate on the 21st of March we would have called him a false prophet. Nevertheless, when the drum aroused us the next morning at day break we uncovered our heads, stretched our limbs, and the snow rolled down on us we were completely surprised. We were so warm under our extra covering and slept so soundly we were not aware of any change in the weather. It was really ten inches deep and had covered our accoutrements, which were scattered on the ground, so that we had great difficulty in finding them. The clouds passed over and the sun coming out warm soon melted the snow and we had a tiresome march through mud and slush to Mt. Hope, where we met our commissary wagon and prepared to break our fast of 24 hours.

Nothing of interest worth recording occurred during the next week. We moved from place to place and as there was only a small squad of us we usually found good camping grounds, sleeping in vacant stores, ginhouses, etc. The citizens of the neighborhoods and towns where we stopped were glad to have us around for protection from the raiding parties which frequently came out from Decatur. They divided liberally with us the subsistence which they had saved by hiding in thickets and secluded places, so we fared well and the only hindrance to our enjoyment was the longing to cross the river and visit homefolk once more.

---

* *See Serial 57, pages 626–627, report of Colonel Jackson.* Ed.

Furloughed, Finally

Colonel Jackson had sympathized with us ever since the other companies were furloughed, but feared we might be captured and he would have to bear the censure. On March 28th, he announced that he had decided to take the risk. He cautioned us to be very watchful and exacted a promise that each of us would report back promptly on expiration of our furloughs. These remarks were greeted with cheers and of course we were willing to make any kind of promise required.

We were disbanded and every fellow allowed to make his way home as best he could. The three Lauderdale Companies were made up above and below Florence, extending a distance of over forty miles parallel with the river. Consequently, we soon began to break off into small squads, separating as we reached points opposite our homes.

The greatest difficulty we encountered was the means of crossing the river which was half a mile wide, and crafts of all kinds were very scarce and no ferries in operation. After a long search, I found an old man who owned a canoe. Although a Union man, he very kindly ferried me over. I was then four miles from home and took a "bee line" through the woods to avoid any Federals who might be passing.

I am sure I will be pardoned for narrating a few personal reminiscences of my visit home as the experience of other members of the regiment who lived inside the enemy's lines were similar to mine. It will serve to give the reader a faint idea of the indignities to which the people of that section were subjected for three long years.

Arriving home late in the afternoon of the second day, I was at once informed that I was in great danger of being captured, that squads and companies of Federals were passing almost every day and the "Tories", as they were called, made frequent raids, robbing and plundering the citizens and murdering Confederate soldiers who might be so unfortunate as to fall into their hands. These men were mostly Tennesseeans, but I regret to say a few were Alabamians. They had their headquarters in the hills of Tennessee and operated in parties of 20, 30 and sometimes as many as a hundred or more. They wore the Blue, not for love of the Union, but for protection of the Federal army, behind whose lines they hovered, not having the manhood to go to the front and never being seen near a battlefield. They make war on women and old men, and in fact were nothing more than a band of thieves and murderers, for they did not hesitate to kill citizens as well as soldiers, when it suited their purpose to do so. They tortured old men, who were supposed to have money, in every conceivable way, by hanging, burning or whipping, as they thought most likely to induce them to give up their money.

In view of the peril of my position, one of the first things to be attended to was to plan some way of escape when it should become necessary. The family had a hiding place for provisions and valuables which they had used two years and it had never been discovered. A section large enough to admit a man's body was sawed out of the ceiling of a small back room and could only be entered by placing a chair on a table and climbing in from the chair.

We put out a sentinel to watch for the Yankees, but the first night passed without an alarm. The next day our faithful old servant, who was on picket, ran in the house and said, "Hide quick, the Tories are coming." On looking out I saw about forty coming at a gallop and by the time I could crawl in and have my sister remove the chair, I heard the clanging of sabres and rattle of spurs in the room below me. The room was low and only a thin ceiling between us, so I could hear distinctly every word spoken. In some way they had learned I was home, and the first inquiry was for me, which surprised me very much when I heard my name called. In my haste to hide, I left my $75.00 hat in the room, and one of them seized it saying he knew it was mine, but a young lady visitor snatched it from his head and saved it. They searched every nook and corner and when they despaired of finding me, began to pillage, all the time using the most vile and profane language. It made my blood boil to hear my mother and sisters insulted by the thieving scoundrels, but I could do nothing, and had to stand it. They stayed about an hour and left in the direction of Florence.

When I came down I found such a wreck as I had never before witnessed. The contents of trunks, drawers and wardrobes were scattered over the house and yard. Women's clothes and such articles as they didn't want were trampled under the feet of men and horses, many of them utterly ruined. We gathered up the fragments and I was told that this was a common occurrence and nothing better was expected when they made their visits.

The next day the same gang came on their return trip. I was warned in time to get into my place of retreat, and the same scenes were re-enacted as on the day before. They searched for me again and volunteered the threat that I should never recross the Tennessee River. After abusing the family to their heart's content and stealing everything of value they failed to get the day before, they left for the hills of Tennessee with the plunder they had secured.

The following day the tramp of cavalry was heard before they came in sight, so I had plenty of time to reach my hiding place. This was quite a large company and a portion of them dismounted, others holding their horses. When I heard their voices I recognized them as real Yankees and felt some consolation that if captured by them the worst to befall me would be term in prison. What might have been my fate if so unfortunate as to fall into the hands of the Tories I could only conjecture, but judging from the history of the gang it was very probable the Confederacy would have been short one soldier. The company made a brief stay and left without molesting anything or anybody.

Having been cooped up in the house three days hardly daring to step outside the door and in continuous suspense, I determined to take to the woods and spend the nights at home. My sister suggested a plan which, when carried out, proved to be very pleasant. There were several of my company in the neighborhood and word was passed from house to house for all the boys and girls to meet in a certain secluded place, away from the public road to spend the day. The girls prepared nice things to eat and the first day's outing was enjoyed so much, we unanimously agreed to meet again the next day. The result was that a succession of picnics followed and we had a delightful time. Our sweethearts dressed in homespun and wheat straw hats which we thought looked prettier and sweeter than before the war when they wore silks and laces. Ladies of wealth and refinement, who had never done manual labor, had learned to spin and weave cotton cloth which, when made up and trimmed with taste, was quite becoming. It was impossible to procure Northern manufactured goods, and indeed was considered unpatriotic to wear them if they could be had. So the women ripped and turned their old dresses until worn out and it was a matter of necessity to accept the homespun styles.

The Federals were scouting around in the vicinity every day and we had some quite narrow escapes, but successfully eluded them until the last day. We had just separated about sundown and were wending our way to our respective homes, when a squad of Yankees swooped down on a party of three girls and two of the boys. The girls were released and the boys carried to camps twelve miles away, arriving at midnight. Guarded till morning, they were arraigned before the commanding officer and actually "lied" themselves out of the scrape. One of them had been discharged in 1861 on account of a wound received at 1st Manassas, but at that time belonged to a cavalry command. He produced his discharge and told the Colonel he had never been in the army since. The other was a member of my company and my chum and classmate. When his turn came he said he had never been a soldier and never would be. His youthful appearance was much in his favor and after some further investigation both of them were released.

Capture of a Federal Cavalry Company

Our furloughs expired on April 7th and, having previously made arrangements for crossing the river, I started back to Mt. Hope where we were ordered to assemble. Although I had enjoyed my visit home my mind had been in constant strain and I felt great relief when I landed on the Confederate side of the river. Arriving at Mt. Hope, I found about 100 of the boys comfortably quartered in vacant houses, and arrivals the next few days brought the number up to 125. All of them made similar reports that they had been harassed by the enemy and compelled to "hide out" during the whole time, the county being patrolled by detached companies, who were stationed at different points from which they made daily raids. One battalion was camped at Colonel Jackson's farm seven miles north of the river and when the Colonel proposed to cross over in the night and take them in it met with a ready response. We thought it would be a good joke on them and a satisfaction to us to retaliate to some extent for the annoyance they had caused us. It required but a short time for us to be ready to move out and by a brisk march we arrived at Tuscumbia Landing at three p.m. the next day. This was opposite the seven mile island and we found ourselves in a dilemma. If we crossed above the island we would be so near Florence the enemy, of whom there was a considerable force, would discover us and frustrate our plans. To have gone below would have landed us ten or twelve miles from our destination and we could not make the trip and return by daylight, so it was decided to ferry all into the island and, under cover of night, row the boat around the upper point. Everything worked smoothly except that we had a very inferior, old, flat boat which was capable of carrying only a few men at a time, but by patience and hard work the last were landed—still seven miles from our destination.

The difficulty that now confronted us was that we could not possibly make the trip to the Jackson place and return by daylight and, in case of failure to do this, the enemy would have time to gather forces from Florence and other places, cut off and capture us. Colonel Jackson said he did not feel like taking so much responsibility on himself because if it should result disastrously, he would have to bear the censure. We were loath to give up the expedition and while parleying over the matter Colonel Ives struck a trail which led us in another direction. He found an old darkey who informed him that the "White Horse" Company was camped on the Peters plantation four miles distant. Pressing the old negro to act as guide, we proceeded to feel our way through the dark bottom, which was accomplished with the loss of valuable time, but once in the open country we got along very well by the light of the stars. When we sighted the campfires we were halted and formed in line. The Colonel instructed us to move slowly with the least possible noise until he gave the command, "Charge", then to fire into the camp, yelling, "Forrest."

All were asleep except a few sentinels pacing their beats, feeling such security that they had neglected to place any guards, except immediately around their camps. When within 150 yards of the camp, the command, "Charge 'em boys!", rang out on the clear night air and, after a volley, we rushed upon them. They ran into a large barn and began firing through cracks and windows, but it was only a few moments until we had them surrounded and they begged for quarter.

When the excitement subsided we learned we had captured the "White Horse" company of the 9th Ohio cavalry. This regiment had uniform horses, one company white, another black, bay, etc. We got 42 men, 44 white horses, 20 or 30 mules, a lot of fine guns and pistols, besides a number of cattle which they had collected and intended driving off the next day. We turned the cattle loose, hoping they would find the way back to their owners. The casualties were four Yankees and one Confederate all killed, no wounded. We tarried but a short time believing that it was important for us to get back on our side of the river as early as possible, as a small force could have prevented us crossing or at least delay us until they could gather a larger force.

We reached the river at sunrise and first ferried everything onto the island, swimming horses and mules by the side of the boat. Then we pursued the same plan as the night before, landing prisoners and at 3 p.m. the next day, we learned that the enemy, believing Forrest was after them, sent out couriers to all the Federals in the county, the 9th Ohio, 7th Illinois, and perhaps others, and had them concentrate in Florence where they began fortifying. If we had known they were so badly demoralized we need not have made such haste in our return to the river.*

We detailed 30 men to escort the prisoners to Tuscaloosa, where they were turned over to the authorities and, from letters received from some of them since the war, I learned they were sent to Cahaba, Alabama and later to Andersonville

---

* For confirmation of the events given of the capture of a Federal cavalry company, see Serial 57, pages 662–663, report of Colonel Ives. Ed.

where they remained to the close of the war. After this little affair, we spent the intervening time, till the last of the month, in different towns in the valley, the greater portion in Courtland where we were quartered in vacant storehouses and received such kind treatment from the citizens, especially the ladies, that we have ever since held them in grateful remembrance.

Back to the War

On April 29, 1864, the order which we had been expecting came for us to report to General Joseph E. Johnston in Georgia, and the next day we started on a long march "to the war" again. Our recruiting expedition proved a failure. Those who had patriotism enough to fight for their country had joined other commands long before and those who had not were lying out in the thickets or had refuged North. We gained a few recruits, but lost as many by capture, so we started back with about the same number we had when we left Demopolis. We ascended the Sand Mountain through Days Gap, some forty miles east of the point where we had come into the valley. From thence our route lay through a very rough, poor country and a majority of the people sympathized with the enemy, but were not so hostile and we found more Southern sentiment than in the mountainous region further west. Being somewhat short of rations we depended partly on foraging, but the country was so poor that subsistence was very scarce. The people seemed willing enough to sell us anything they had to spare, but positively refused to take our Confederate money. They would take Alabama state money which was "payable in Confederate", but we had none and were able to convince them that one was as good as the other.

The march to Montevallo consumed seven days and was without incident worth mentioning. On arrival there, we found part of the army of Mississippi moving towards Georgia, but our brigade had just left again, so we fell in with Featherstone's brigade and a three day march brought us to Rome, Georgia. We then boarded a train and reached Resaca at 2 a.m. on May 12th, where we overtook our command. It seemed almost like home to be with the old brigade once more, but some changes had taken place since we left it. The 3rd, 7th and 8th Kentucky had been mounted and under General Buford were then with Forrest.

Colonel Thomas M. Scott of the 12th Louisiana commanded the brigade, Loring the division, and Polk the corps.

We were immediately placed in line of battle and began throwing up breastworks, as Sherman was flanking Johnston at Dalton, and it was certain our forces would fall back to Resaca. This was the beginning of the 100 days fighting in the Georgia campaign, and having kept a diary at that time, which gives our movements in detail, perhaps better than I could do now. I will quote from it omitting such parts as have no bearing on the history of the regiment.

Forward to Diary Entries

The brigade of Colonel T. M. Scott as formed on June 10, 1864 consisted of these regiments: 27th Alabama, under Colonel James Jackson; 35th Alabama, under Colonel S. S. Ives; 49th Alabama, under Lieutenant Colonel John D. Weeden; 55th Alabama under Colonel John Snodgrass; 57th Alabama, under Colonel Charles J. L. Cunningham; and 12th Louisiana, under Lieutenant Colonel Noel L. Nelson, in Loring's division, Polk's corps. See Serial 74, page 645.

J. P. Cannon Diary Entries

FRIDAY, MAY 13, 1864:

Our forces evacuated Dalton last night and are in retreat. A large force of the enemy reported to be moving on Resaca. At 10 a.m. our brigade was ordered to the front to feel of them and watch their movements. We went two miles or more without finding any Yanks, and began to think it was a false alarm, when emerging from the woods into a wheat field, we were suddenly greeted with a shower of bullets from the opposite side of the field.

We were ordered to lie down, but that order was unnecessary, as we were already down. As our guns were loaded we returned the compliment at once. In a few minutes, the firing became general from one end of the brigade to the other and we realized that we had got into a mighty hot place.

We kept up the fight for an hour or two, neither side showing any disposition to advance, without much loss on our side, as we were pretty well protected behind logs, trees, and stumps.

During the heat of the battle an incident occurred which caused some merriment to those of us who were near enough to see and hear what was going on. When we were ordered to the front this morning our Chaplain, who is a valiant soldier of the cross but had never been in a battle, said he wanted to go with us. So we gave him an Enfield rifle and strapped a cartridge-box around him and at the command he fell into line.

When the firing began he took position behind a stump and "lit into them" with all his might. Having fired a half-dozen or more rounds, Lt. Chandler said: "Parson, let me rest you a while; I want to shoot some". He handed the gun to the Lieutenant and C. began to load and shoot,while the parson squatted behind him. In a short time he got restless, as any soldier will when exposed to the fire of an enemy, with nothing to do but listen to the zip, zip of bullets as they flit past or

64

the loud screech of the shells that seem like they are going to take the top of his head off when they are probably a hundred feet away. He has an impediment in his speech and stammers very badly when excited, and no doubt this was one of the most exciting experiences of his life. He stood it a short time and reaching out towards the gun said:

"J-J-J-Jim, g-g-g-give me my g-g-g-gun."

"Hold on a little, " said Jim.

The parson waited impatiently, no doubt thinking it a long time, and—"J-J-J-Jim, I m-m-m-must have my g-g-g-gun."

By this time those when were near by had become very much interested, and watched the parson about as much as we did the Yankees. He continued to grow more excited and impatient, first lying down, then squatting behind Jim, then standing and cutting up all sort of capers. The next break he made for his gun and said:

"J-J-J-Jim, if you d-d-d-don't g-g-g-give me my g-g-g-gun, I c-c-c-can't stay here."

"Lie down and be still."

"I c-c-c-can't lie d-d-d-down. I m-m-m-must h-h-h-have my g-g-g-gun."

Jim kept firing and finally, his patience being exhausted, the parson said, "J-J-J-Jim, I c-c-c-can't s-s-s-stand it any l-l-l-longer, I'm go-g-g-going to the r-r-r-r-r-"—all the time moving down the hill. Before he could pronounce the word "rear" Jim called him back and gave him his gun. He got behind his stump and was soon loading and firing as coolly as a veteran and continued to do so until the enemy was reinforced and compelled our little brigade to "skedaddle."

We had a "running fight" back to our line-of-battle, which had been formed in front of the town, where we prepared for the expected attack, by piling logs, rails, and anything we could find for temporary breastworks, our position being in a swamp, where the mud and water were ankle deep.

It wasn't long before skirmishing began all along the line, and at 3 p.m. our pickets were driven in and we could see a dark line of blue moving toward us. Raising a hurrah, they started at a double-quick, but one volley broke their line and they fell back in confusion. In a short time, the same movement was repeated and a second repulse followed. The third time they rallied, but we poured such a storm of shot and shell into them that their ranks were broken and they fell back disheartened.

This ended the fight for the day, after which we got picks and spades and went to work with a determination to be better prepared for an assault that might reasonably be expected in the morning. We worked faithfully in mud and water till near midnight, feeling that our lives might be the forfeit if we failed to make our works bullet proof; and with such an incentive who would not work?

About midnight we prepared for a little sleep and those who were able to get a piece of plank or a couple of rails to keep them out of the mud were lucky indeed.

SATURDAY, MAY 14, 1864: Resaca, Georgia

The night passed quietly. We got a few hours good sleep and felt very refreshed. The troops from Dalton had arrived and all are in good spirits, ready to do their duty when General Johnston, in whom we have the utmost confidence, says the time has come to fight.

There was skirmishing all day along the entire line. On the right several fierce assaults were made and gallantly repulsed by our boys. We have been watching and waiting for an advance in our front all day, but they don't seem inclined to repeat the experiment of yesterday.

At sunset the artillery opened all along the line from both sides. It was grand and terrific. For miles to the right and left the cannons belched forth their thunder until 9 o'clock, when gradually they ceased, and everything became quiet except the continual bang of the pickets, which was kept up without intermission all night.

SUNDAY, MAY 15, 1864: Resaca, Georgia

The "Day of Rest" opened bright and beautiful and we expected a general engagement would take place between the two armies now confronting each other, but we were disappointed. I never saw more enthusiasm among our soldiers or more eagerness for battle. General Johnston has infused new life into the army and we feel that now is the time to retrieve the misfortunes which have befallen us in the past and if we can meet Sherman on anything like an equal footing we have no fears of the result. Why we did not have a general battle today I have no means of knowing, but presume that each commander is waiting for the other to make the attack.

Several minor engagements took place during the day. In the forenoon, the Yankees attempted to take possession of the railroad bridge and after a short but fierce little battle we drove them off. A number of attacks were made on different points of our line, which were handsomely repulsed with considerable loss to the enemy. Late in the evening a very determined assault was made on Stephenson's division of our corps.

It was very exciting to those of us who were not engaged watching line after line of blue as they moved forward with a hurrah, but our boys stood firm, driving them back and leaving many of them on the field.

We have spent all our leisure time between fights in strengthening our works, working in mud and water from "shoe mouth" to knee deep. When night closed the conflicts of the day we felt that we were better prepared to resist the attack which we hope will be made tomorrow.

After eating supper, which consisted of a small corn-dodger and piece of bacon, we lay down to rest with nothin to disturb us except the firing of the pickets, which extended as far as we could hear, both on the right or left.

MONDAY, MAY 16, 1864:

We got to sleep but a few short hours last night. At 1 o'clock we were roused and formed into line (not line of battle but line of retreat) to our great surprise and regret, for we had hoped to defeat Sherman today and drive him back at least to the Tennessee River.

It is reported that we are largely outnumbered and it must be true or General Johnston certainly would have made a determined stand, for he will never have an army in better condition or more eager for the fray.

From the best information I can get we have about 45,000 men and the report is that Sherman has at least 100,000. If this is correct it is better to fall back, and we have so much confidence in Old Joe that we are willing to be guided by his judgement and wait until he says the time has come to strike.

We marched all night and crossed the Oostanaula River at daylight, burning the bridges behind us, passed through Calhoun and three miles south of that town were halted and ordered to rest in place. The enemy made an attack on Hood's Corps and were repulsed, which was the only fighting of the day.

TUESDAY, MAY 17, 1864: Near Calhoun, Ga.

We "slept on arms" last night, getting a good night's rest, and continued the retreat this morning. Our division being rear-guard, we had our hands full today. Continually pressed by the enemy, we often had to stop and check them, then double-quick to overtake the rest of the command, but our loss has been very light considering the number of tight places we got into during the day.

At Adairsville we were halted, formed in line-of-battle and ordered to rest, which we very much needed. The Yankees attacked Hardee's Corps, but were repulsed. We are victorious in every battle, but still we have to retreat. There is no doubt that Sherman has an army largely in excess of ours in our front and send 30,000 to 40,000 men around one of our flanks, which compels us to retreat; but we are not discouraged yet.

We hope, by forcing him to attack us under disadvantages as he has been doing for some days, and drawing him into the interior, farther from his base, that we can eventually weaken him until we can risk a general engagement.

WEDNESDAY, MAY 18, 1864: Near Cassville, Ga.

We left Adairsville last night at 10 o'clock and had a dreary, tiresome march all night arriving at Cassville at daylight and "slept on arms" till 9 a.m., then moved half a mile and formed a new line.

Our company was detailed as skirmishers, and we had a lively time the balance of the day, but being in the timber we all took shelter behind trees and a six hour battle resulted in very little loss to either side. We were relieved early in the night and returned to the line-of-battle, but the pickets kept up a ceaseless firing as long as we remained awake.

General Johnston sent around a circular complimenting the troops upon their steadiness and faithfulness on the battlefield and on retreat. He said we have repulsed every assault, that we are weakening the enemy and strengthening ourselves every time we fall back and the time will shortly come when we will make a stand and he expects every man to be at his post and do his whole duty.

FRIDAY, MAY 20, 1864:

We had to skedaddle again last night, passing through Cartersville and across the Etowah River; marched all night till 12 o'clock today when we stopped and formed in line-of-battle. The Yankees followed closely and almost by the time we got ready they were in line, confronting us and the pickets commenced their same old pastime.

Since this campaign opened, all the cooking has been done in the rear by men detailed for that purpose, as we have had no time for cooking, having been in line-of-battle or on the retreat since the 12th of May. The usual picket fighting and sharp-shooting has been going on all day, but nothing of importance occurred. Two hundred Yankees crossed the river on a reconnoitering expedition, but were captured without a fight.

MONDAY, MAY 23, 1864: "Way down in Georgia"

We had a fair night's sleep and got up wondering what would be the program for the day. At 10 a.m. we commenced "advancing backward" again and moved in the direction of Marietta; had a hot, dusty, and disagreeable march all day, stacked arms and camped in line-of-battle.

Rations are getting very scarce. We are getting about enough cornbread and bacon for one meal. This constitutes a day's rations. Lt. Chandler slipped out on a foraging expedition during the march, and came in at night with an armful of cornbread, which we enjoyed very much in the absence of anything better. Jim says there is nothing to eat in the country and he is the best forager in the regiment. When he fails, no one else need try.

TUESDAY, MAY 24, 1864:

We were roused before daylight and continued our retreat. We marched till 4 p.m. formed in line and were ordered to "rest on arms." Skirmishing and cannonading have been quite heavy all day. Yanks lined up in our front and opened on us with artillery, then the pickets joined in; but we are getting used to such rackets and did not lose much sleep on account of it.

WEDNESDAY, MAY 25, 1864:

We maneuvered so much all the morning, going backward, then forward, by the right flank and by the left flank, forming line-of-battle here, then moving to another position, that it was hard to tell whether we were to attack the enemy or expecting to be attacked. In the meantime, we could hear heavy firing on the extreme left, which gradually approached nearer and nearer until it reached Hood's Corps, at which time we were immediately ordered to the scene of action on a double-quick.

The roar of musketry and boom of artillery mingled together told plainly that blood was being spilled freely and with a yell we pressed on to let Hood's boys know that help was near and encourage them to stand to their posts. Before we reached the battleground stray bullets began to strike in our ranks and several were killed and wounded.

Just in rear of Hood's line, we were halted and found that both sides were merely holding their own. We rested a few minutes, and somewhat recovered our breath, when we were ordered forward. Then came the "tug of war." The Yanks contested the ground stubbornly, and the carnage was fearful, but slowly they yielded till night set in and put an end to the struggle, leaving us in possession of the battlefield amid the groans of the wounded and dying, which was more distressing than the ordeal through which we had just passed.

We gave such assistance to our fallen comrades and foes as we could till 11 o'clock, when we were ordered to "fall in" and marched and counter-marched through thickets and swamps, the rain pouring down on us in torrents the remainder of the night. At daylight, we halted and, lying down in our wet clothes, welcomed sleep that soon blotted out the remembrances of the day and night.

THURSDAY, MAY 26, 1864: Near New Hope Church

Lt. Olive came in this morning with a squad of our boys who were left in the enemy's line in Alabama. They brought us letters which is the first news we have had from home since we left there.

A spirit of liberality seems to have struck our Commissary. He sent us two days' rations equal to any four that we have received since the campaign opened. Our rations have been very short for two weeks and consisted only of hard corn dodgers and bacon; but we do not complain, because we know it is the best they can do for us, as long as the enemy holds so much of our territory.

In the afternoon the Yankees moved up and skirmishing began in our front. We formed general line-of-battle and went to work. We are getting to be expert with pick and spade and it does not take long to dig a ditch two or three feet deep, throwing the dirt in front which protects us from the bullets and fragments of shells which are continually flying around and about us.

FRIDAY, MAY 27, 1864:

Skirmishing and cannonading continued all night and became general all around the line this morning. It begins to look like we are to make a stand at last. We have been retreating for three weeks, yet we are cheerful and in high spirits. Usually an army becomes demoralized when it has to fall back continually, but we have enough confidence in our commander to believe that when the opportunity comes he will strike the enemy a blow which will stop his aggressive movements; at any rate, we are ready to fight or retreat when he gives the command.

No battle occurred during the day except that Cleburne's division was attacked by several lines that were repulsed with heavy loss and Cleburne, taking advantage of their confusion, charged and drove them from their works.

SATURDAY, MAY 28, 1864:

Early last night our division had to move half a mile to the right and from the movements of the enemy, we expected a night attack, but nothing more than skirmishing and cannonading occurred. We had to sleep in the ditch as the Yankees are so close to us that it is dangerous to be above ground.

They are fortified about 250 yards in our front and the pickets had to come in as soon as it got light enough to see. We have been confined in the ditch all day, amusing ourselves by shooting at the Yanks every time we could see one, and getting shot at when we dared to raise our heads above the breastworks.

Hardee's Corps was attacked with the usual result. The enemy were driven back and must have suffered severely. We are certainly reducing their strength, as they charge some part of our works every day, which reasonably makes their loss much heavier than ours and we have repulsed every attack (so far as I know) since we left Dalton.

SUNDAY, MAY 29, 1864: Near New Hope Church

Another bright Sabbath day was ushered in amid the thunder of artillery and rattle of musketry along a line probably eight or 10 miles in length. It was kept up the same way all night and we slept in the ditches again, bullets continually whizzing over us. Being securely sheltered no harm was done except occasionally when a fragment of shell would strike some poor fellow who was unfortunate enough to have made his bed in an unlucky spot.

Both sides are well fortified and so close together that no pickets are used in day time, but at night a line of sentries are placed in front of the works to prevent a surprise, while the remainder sleep in the ditches. During the day a harassing fire kept up from the breastworks, resulting in a small loss, but causing us (and the Yankees, too) to "lay low."

When details are made to go for water or other purposes, they draw the fire of hundreds of guns from the opposite side and although quite serious to them, sometimes it is right amusing to see them run and dodge until they get shelter behind a hill or so far into the timber that they cannot be seen.

We have been annoyed a great deal by a battery just left of our front, and General Loring called for volunteers to make an assault on it at midnight. He said it was a hazardous undertaking and he wanted none but brave, determined men to volunteer.

MONDAY, MAY 30, 1864:

The attack on the battery was abandoned. I do not know why, but presume it was considered the sacrifice was too great for the good to be accomplished.

Last night our turn came for picket duty, 30 of our company being detailed for that purpose under command of Captain Thompson. We were ordered to proceed 100 yards to the front, deploy to the right 10 paces apart, so as to cover the front of our regiment, and cautioned to be as quiet as possible. Any noise would provoke an attack from the breastworks, which would be only 150 yards from us.

We reached the designated place without any mishap, but in filing to the right some of the boys got tangled in a brush pile, making considerable racket, which the Yankees probably mistook for a forward movement and without warning, boom!

boom! boom!, a battery of six guns not more than 200 yards distant opened on us and fairly shook the earth.

The thunder of the first volley had scarcely died away when the infantry rose from their trenches and a sheet of flame burst from their ranks, extending as far as we could see in either direction. This was followed by artillery all along the line and from then on it was a ceaseless roar. It reminded us of one of the roaring winds, the flashes of lightning and heavy peals of thunder in a terrible storm.

The night was dark, but the woods above and around us were ablaze with burning fuses and bursting shells, while the limbs were cut off and falling from the trees and the air was thick with hissing minie-balls. Five thousand guns and 20 cannon shooting right into our little squad of 30 men! Would they ever cease? Would one of us be left to tell the tale? These were some of the questions which were thought, if not asked aloud.

At the first flash of the guns, we all dropped prone upon the ground and for 40 minutes (it seemed very much longer) they kept up the most incessant and terrific fire I ever heard.

When everything became perfectly quiet, we moved out very cautiously, deploying 10 feet apart and had a lonely watch all night long. As dawn began to appear in the east, we silently withdrew to the breastworks, made our beds in the ditch, and were soon asleep. We got up about 12 o'clock, but had to remain under cover the remainder of the day.

TUESDAY, MAY 31, 1864:

All is quiet on our part of the line and we got a good night's sleep. Nothing occurred during the day worth recording, except a charge of Featherstone's brigade. The Federals attempted to advance their line and Featherstone charged and drove them back.

WEDNESDAY, JUNE 1, 1864: In the Ditches

Another month has passed and no general engagement, though a number of battles have been fought, with the advantage largely on our side. We have generally fought under cover and have inflicted a loss of at least three to one, but Sherman, having such a large force, can flank and compel us to fall back when it suits him to do so.

Our hopes to reduce his strength before reaching Atlanta, so we can give him battle with something near an equal force. If we can do this we feel sure of a great victory. Skirmishing has been brisk all around the line today wherever they have pickets, but we are still so close together that all the firing is done from the breastworks.

THURSDAY, JUNE 2, 1864:

We put our pickets as usual last night, and settled ourselves in the ditches for a good night's sleep, but at 1 o'clock the Yanks made it so hot for them that they had to run in, and we joined in and had a lively time for an hour or more. The artillery "took a hand" and we wasted enough ammunition to have fought a big battle, but very little damage was done, as both lines were sheltered by good breastworks. After the battle ceased, we finished our nap and have spent the day as usual.

FRIDAY, JUNE 3, 1864:

It rained very hard last night and filled our ditch half full of water, so we are wet, muddy, and hungry, rations being very short, but the boys say this is the way to "git your independence." Sharp-shooting and occasional firing from the breastworks continued through the day.

SATURDAY, JUNE 4, 1864:

Our turn came again last night to go on picket-line, and we had a more quiet time than we did the last time. The Yanks behaved very well and the Captain did not have to admonish us a single time "not to go to sleep." We came in before daylight and spent the day in the muddy ditches, the rain still pouring down.

SUNDAY, JUNE 5, 1864:

At dark last night, the artillery commenced moving, and at 11 o'clock the infantry (except two regiments from each brigade) were ordered to fall in and we moved out to the right. The night was dark and dreary, rain still falling, but we groped our way through woods, fields, and muddy roads till daylight, when we halted in line and remained during the day.

MONDAY, JUNE 6, 1864: Near Lost Mountain, Ga.

The enemy are moving on our right toward Marietta and we have done considerable maneuvering.

TUESDAY, JUNE 7, 1864:

Clear and bright the sun shone out warm and dried our wet clothes, which have been thoroughly soaked for three days and nights. Our corps moved four miles to the right, getting into several skirmishes, but no serious engagement.

WEDNESDAY, JUNE 8, 1864:

All was quiet last night, and we got a good night's sleep. We moved to the right again, the right wing of our brigade now resting on the railroad, three miles north of Marietta. Cannonading and skirmishing at intervals all day.

THURSDAY, JUNE 9, 1864:

We have had a busy day, moving from point to point, often in double-quick; got into several sharp skirmishes in which we lost quite a number of men and finally formed a general line-of-battle, the line running through a citizen's yard, our company's position being half-way between his house and front gate.

The Yanks moved up very promptly and by the time we had our line fairly well established, their skirmishers were popping away at us, and the bullets, coming zip, zip made it uncomfortable, the more so as we were in the open yard with not a tree or stump to get behind. Having no tools, we began piling up rails, logs, etc. for temporary protection until we could get picks and spades to make something better.

FRIDAY, JUNE 10, 1864:

It rained last night and continued today. We got picks and spades and went to work in earnest, digging ditches to protect us more effectually. Skirmishing has been brisk all day, and cannonading part of the time, but no engagement worth of being called a battle. Hood's Corps is massed on the right, ours (Polk's) in the center, and Hardee on the left.

SATURDAY, JUNE 11, 1864:

Rain! Rain! Rain! Rain! It has rained so much the last few days that operations of both armies are retarded, though nothing it seems can stop the everlasting sharpshooting and skirmishing.

SUNDAY, JUNE 12, 1864:

It is a gloomy Sunday; clouds dark and rain still pouring down. We have not been dry for three days and have been compelled to stay in the freshly dug ditches, where the water collects in puddles. Muddy from head to foot, we present a pitiable spectacle. We have not had a wash-day since we left north Alabama— six weeks ago.

TUESDAY, JUNE 14, 1864:

"Old Sol" came out bright and we greeted him with cheers. At 2 p.m. we moved to the right and relieved Hood's Corps, taking possession of their ditches. We were glad to do so, as it saves us considerable hard work, the first thing these times being to get a hole in the ground as speedily as possible. We are stretched out in one rank, to cover as much ground as possible, so as to give Hood an opportunity of meeting the flank movement of Sherman on our right.

When our grub-wagon came in today, as usual, we made a rush for it. In addition to the customary hard corn dodgers and bacon we found a small sack, the contents of which were entirely new to us. All agreed that it resembled something we had seen "before the war" and quite a lively discussion ensued.

One said, "It's Yankee peas," another that it was "Boston beans," and various opinions were expressed, causing a good deal of merriment, until Joe Clanton (who talks as through his nose) says, "Boys, ain't you all got a darned bit of sense? I'm ashamed of you'n. That's gin-u-wine Lincoln coffee." That settled the matter and we proceeded to divide it; but how to divide so small a quantity among a whole regiment was puzzling.

However, we surmounted the difficulty by making 10 little parcels (one for each company), then subdividing to the messes, which reduced it to so small a quantity that we had to count the grains, resulting in the magnificent sum of 50 grains to each man.

Our fun over the coffee was soon changed to mourning. Our corps commander, the Christian soldier, General Polk, was struck in the breast by a cannonball and instantly killed. It was a great shock to the Army of the Mississippi, which he organized and had commanded since the fall of Vicksburg. We all loved him and had great confidence in him as commander; but, great as the calamity is, it is the fortunes of war, and we must submit.

WEDNESDAY, JUNE 15, 1864: Near Kenesaw Mountain, Ga.

We moved to the foot of Kenesaw. Our brigade was placed on a hill and ordered to hold it at all hazards. Here we have a splendid view of both armies. On the right and left can be seen the Confederates, clad in many colors, butternut jeans predominating, all more or less bespattered with the red Georgia mud from the fresh ditches.

In front, a long line of blue extending for miles in either direction, their bright arms glistening in the sunlight presenting a grand spectacle.

The contrast in appearance of the contending forces, the arms and munitions of war, is indeed very great; but if we can ever meet them with equal numbers, we feel that we can overcome the disparity in other respects and retrieve the misfortunes of the past in a glorious victory.

We have had heavy skirmishing most all day, our brigade has lost as many men as we sometimes lose in a pitched battle. Between skirmishes we put in the time "throwing dirt" with a vim, in order to be prepared for any emergency which might arise.

General Loring has taken General Polk's place, and now commands the Army of the Mississippi.

THURSDAY, JUNE 16:

Our men worked by details all night and this morning found us with fair breastworks and an impregnable position, one that can stand the assaults of Sherman's hosts indefinitely. His only chance to dislodge us is by another flank movement, which I have no doubt he will be able to accomplish with the superior force he has at hand.

Musketry and cannonading was kept up all night and continued today, which, with the sharpshooting, has annoyed us a great deal. The enemy charged Cleburne's division, but were repulsed with heavy loss.

FRIDAY, JUNE 17, 1864:

Nothing worth recording, more than the regular picket fighting, sharpshooting, and an occasional artillery duel.

SATURDAY, JUNE 18, 1864:

Our regiment went on picket early last night and stood all night in drenching rain. Just before day, our company was moved forward about 300 yards in front of the regiment, deployed 10 paces apart, and ordered to keep a close watch, as the enemy was nearby; and, indeed, we soon found that such was the case. As soon as it got light enough we could see their picket-line less than 100 yards from us, and saluting each other "good morning," both sides took such cover as was at hand, behind trees, logs, stumps, etc. We had a "hide and seek" game all the morning, firing every time we could get a glimpse of each other, and several of our boys got wounded, one very seriously.

About 2 p.m. a squad of 15 or 20 Yankees crawled down a ravine and got possession of a log house half way between the lines. This exposed those of us who were on the right of the house, to cross-fire, and our trees were not large enough to cover us in front and flank at the same time. When we dodged from one we were exposed to the other and vice versa.

It was the worst scrape I ever got into, and I had rather take my chances in a regular battle than another such. They made it so hot that something had to be done, and that very quickly, or we couldn't stay there; so we sent a courier back and reported the situation to Colonel Jackson, who very promptly brought up a detachment from the regiment, charged the house and drove the Yankees back to their picket-line, much to our great relief and delight; but it cost us several casualties.

Colonel Jackson had his arm shattered above the elbow, so it will have to be amputated. The Colonel was shot through the chest at first Manassas, when a private in the 4th Alabama, on account of which wound he was discharged, and afterwards assisted in raising the 27th Alabama with which he has been connected since December 1861.

After dislodging the Yanks from the house, we felt comparatively safe behind our trees, but took good care not to expose ourselves any more than necessary. We spent the remainder of the evening shooting at the Yanks, and they at us, at every opportunity.

SUNDAY, JUNE 19, 1864:

We were relieved from vidette at 2 a.m. and found that we had been all night without any support, the command having left early in the night. We followed and overtook the division at the foot of Kenesaw Mountain, where they had formed another line of battle and were getting out picks and spades, which is always the first thing to be attended to; our regiment, being excused from duty during the day, as we had been on the picket-line two nights and one day, without a "wink" of sleep and most of the time exposed to a heavy rain, which still continues.

MONDAY, JUNE 20, 1864:

Having beds of leaves and brush to keep us out of the water, and stretching blankets over us, we succeeded in getting a few hours sleep in spite of the torrents all night. We felt much refreshed this morning and ready for anything which might come up—especially rations.

When rations came in another surprise was in store for us—both coffee and sugar. Oh! What extravagance! What will become of the Confederate treasury if such recklessness is allowed? Only a week ago we got 50 grains each, and now 110 grains, by actual count, with sugar "to boot."

Colonel Scott, who has been commanding our brigade since General Buford left us, received his commission and is now a full-fledged Brigadier and the 27th, 35th and 49th Alabama were today consolidated. Captain Thompson and Lt. Chandler were retained as line officers of our consolidated company with the regiment now numbering about 600 effectives.

Our present position is at the extreme eastern end of Kenesaw, where the Marietta road curves around the base of the mountain, a hill on the right forming a gap through which the road passes. It is a very important point, for if the enemy could break our line here they could quickly throw a column in the rear of our main army, which occupies the mountain. However, we are well prepared to defend the gap and think we can hold it against any odds.

We have the Point Coupee, a six-gun battery, on the east side of the road and six 24-pound Parrotts on the west side, all posted immediately over our heads. Besides already having pretty fair breastworks, we are continually strengthening them.

The enemy are fortifying a half mile in our front, and the pickets have begun their daily business about half way between the lines. Stray bullets often reach us and even fly high above our heads, but so far, they have done us no harm.

TUESDAY, JUNE 21, 1864:

Our consolidated regiment had to go on picket yesterday evening, and had gone but a short distance when we met the enemy's pickets. A sharp skirmish ensued, each side maneuvering for advantage of position. We charged them and they charged us, having a miniature battle for probably two hours, when night set in and it settled down to the regular bang, bang, which we kept up all night in the rain.

This morning we were relieved and came back to the line, sleepy and wet, and no prospect of getting dry soon. It has rained so much that the roads have become impassable for artillery or wagons, which will probably suspend operations and give us a rest until better weather.

THURSDAY, JUNE 23, 1864:

General A. P. Stewart took command of our corps today, and General Loring resumed command of the division. The battery on our left became so annoying that something must be done, so we opened on them with all the artillery in reach and kept up a furious shelling for probably an hour and a half, after which we assaulted and captured the hill, but failed to get their battery. Our loss, supposed to be about 700, is quite a serious little affair, but we had to get that battery out of the way or there would be no rest for us. There was heavy firing on Hardee's line for two hours; and the news is passed down the line that Hardee repulsed them with heavy loss. We have had a bright, warm day and got thoroughly dry once more.

FRIDAY, JUNE 24, 1864:

The enemy moved up still closer last night and from movements we could see, and the galloping of couriers back and forth, we judged they were preparing for an assault either on us or some other part of the line. Our surmise proved to be correct, for at 11 a.m. heavy firing of both artillery and musketry opened on our left and we saw a line of blue climb over their works and start toward us.

Instantly, every fellow took his place in the ditch, inspecting guns, cartridge-boxes, etc., to see that all was ready. Our 12 guns above our heads turned loose and almost deafened us with their thunder, causing some confusion in the ranks of the enemy. On they came, driving away our pickets, and the command, "Ready, aim, fire," was given, and we poured such a volley into them that they wheeled and retired, leaving quite of number of dead and wounded. But this was only a feint to draw our attention from the left, where the main assault was made, and the battle raged furiously for an hour or more after those in our front were safely in their breastworks. After the battle ceased on our left, we replaced the pickets and remained in the ditches to be ready in case of another attack; but the day passed off quietly, with the exception of the usual skirmishing between the pickets.

SATURDAY, JUNE 25, 1864:

For three hours this morning we had the most quiet time since the campaign opened. Scarcely a gun could be heard; both armies seemed to be in a deep slumber, but it was the "calm before the storm." At 10 a.m. we were awakened by heavy skirmishing in front, and the artillery opened on both sides fast and furious, and old Kenesaw was shaken from "center to circumference." It continued the greater part of the day, but I presume resulted in few casualties on either side.

SUNDAY, JUNE 26, 1864:

The picket fighting was kept up all night and the artillery joined in again early this morning. It seemed as if every battery within range was concentrated on our division, no less than 40 or 50 guns firing directly on us and French's division, which joins us on the left, occupying the eastern slope of the mountain. We thought this was but the prelude to an assault, but when it subsided no demonstration was made by the infantry.

During the cannonade our 12 guns replied vigorously and did some excellent shooting, the thunder of which, so close to our ears and mingled with the screech and noise of bursting bombs all around us, kept us in a state of anxiety and dread; more so than if we had been engaged in actual battle where the danger would have been much greater. An artillery duel is a grand thing when we can view it from some safe place on a distant hill-top, but we fail to appreciate the grandeur of it when directly in range and expecting every moment to be crushed or torn into fragments by one of the horrid shells.

Everything seems to indicate a battle in the near future, and our position is most likely to be one of the points attacked. If so, we are in the best condition we have ever been to receive it.

MONDAY, JUNE 27, 1864:

By daylight the sharpshooters had taken cover in their accustomed places and commenced their deadly work. The skirmishers continued with renewed energy the firing which had been kept up all night. Later, the artillery opened on us and, having previously gotten the range and distance, threw their shells with an accuracy which caused us to lie low in the ditches. Our artillery, being short of ammunition, did not reply much, reserving it for the crisis which all felt would come some time during the day.

At 9 a.m. a roll of musketry broke loose on the left in Hardee's front, gradually extending toward us and in a short time three lines of blue climbed over their works and moved forward. The woods being open timber, mostly tall pines, we could see them plainly from the time they left their works. On they came, maintaining their lines as perfectly as if on division drill, looking formidable enough and outnumbering us three to one. Having largely the advantage, and feeling confidence in our ability to hold our position, we waited patiently for our skirmishers to come in. The 12th Louisiana was on the skirmish-line and stood their ground until the front line of the enemy approached within 25 yards, when they retired. As soon as they were safely inside the breastworks we poured a deadly fire into the face of the advancing foe and at the same time the 12 cannon above us turned loose and grape, canister, and minie-balls mowed them down like grain before the sickle.

Shells and solid shot tore limbs from the trees and split the tall pines like bolts of lightning. They gallantly pressed forward, regardless of the wide gaps which were being cut into their ranks, until the front line was within a stone's throw of our breastworks. When mortal man could stand it no longer, they halted, unable to advance and loath to retreat.

Lying down, they poured volley after volley into us and the fight raged for a full hour when, losing all hope of dislodging us, they retired, leaving many dead and wounded on the field.

Then a cry of victory rose in the throats of the Confederates, carried from one division to another and old Kenesaw resounded with the glad shouts. The enemy's loss must have been very heavy, taking into consideration the disadvantages under which they fought and the number of men engaged. It must have been a general charge, for we could hear the roar of the guns far to the left and on other parts of the line long after they had retired from our front. Our loss was quite small, so far as my observation extended, probably not more than 75 in the brigade.

TUESDAY, JUNE 28, 1864: Kenesaw Mountain

The utter failure of General Sherman to break our line at any point yesterday will have a tendency to make him more cautious in the future, and we may look for a resort to his old tactics, which has heretofore been so successful, that of forcing us to evacuate by a flank movement. It would be recklessness to attempt to dislodge us by direct assault, with all the advantages we have, and he is too good a General to undertake it again.

This has been a rather quiet day with some sharpshooting and an occasional picket fight and cannonade to relieve the monotony, but no change in position of either army, so far as we are able to observe.

WEDNESDAY, JUNE 29, 1864:

Special "telegraphic reports" to another confirm our impression that the enemy's loss on Monday must have been immense, probably 8,000 or 10,000 while ours was comparatively light. A few more engagements like that will reduce Sherman's force so he will not have so many to send around our flanks, and when this desirable result is attained we will offer him battle and believe that a great victory awaits us.

The enemy have been burying their dead under flag-of-truce. A few of us got permission to go out, and Johnny and Yank met on the most friendly terms. We had quite a sociable time, for there is no bad feeling as individuals. Brave men respect each other, no matter how much they differ in opinion.

FRIDAY, JULY 1, 1864:

The month is ushered in with two great armies confronting each other, the lines in many places being less than 100 yards apart, and yet, after an arduous campaign of two months, no decisive battle has been fought. Although we have abandoned one strong position after another, and have been retreating since the 7th of May, the morale of the army is excellent and was never in better condition for battle. Skirmishing has been quite lively all day, both sides reinforcing to such an extent that on many parts of the line it was scarcely less than a battle.

SATURDAY, JULY 2, 1864:

We were aroused at daylight by very heavy firing immediately in our front, it required but a moment for those who were not already in the ditches to take their places and be ready for the supposed attack, but it continued without any advance. The bullets imbedding themselves in our breastworks and singing their little songs over our heads finally dwindled down to a regular picket fight interspersed occasionally with a few rounds from the artillery. This was kept up all day and we had to stay in the ditch or run the risk of being plugged by a stray bullet or piece of shell.

The weather has been oppressively warm, but late in the afternoon a refreshing shower fell and cooled the atmosphere. A short while back we had rain almost every day incessantly for weeks, and hardly thought we would welcome it again in such a short time.

The enemy is flanking us on the left and everything indicates another retrograde movement. Unless we can spare enough men from the ditches to meet and drive back that column we will be compelled to evacuate and place our army between the enemy and Atlanta.

SUNDAY, JULY 3, 1864:

As anticipated, early last night the artillery wheels were wrapped with blankets and rolled away by hand, then the infantry began to move, and Kenesaw Mountain was abandoned. The two lines being so close to each other, it required great secrecy to withdraw without being discovered, but it was accomplished successfully, our regiment being the last to leave the ditches. We felt the necessity of keeping very quiet, even more than those in front, for any intimation to the enemy that we were evacuating would invite an attack, for which we were wholly unprepared. The night was very dark and we had a tiresome march all night till daylight.

July 4th found us still moving toward Atlanta. At 10 a.m. we formed line-of-battle seven miles south of Marietta. The Yanks were "right on our heels," and by the time we had our line established, the skirmishers were engaged. They drove in our skirmishers and, advancing a line of infantry, charged our brigade and Canty's.

Canty's men gave way but seeing us holding our ground they rallied and raising a yell, charged the enemy and recovered their old position. This was quite a sharp little fight, lasting about three-quarters of an hour and we lost several men in the regiment. Captain Thompson, of our company, was shot in the heel, which will disable him for sometime. After the battle, we got picks and spades and went to work, knowing that the quicker we got into the ground the safer we would be.

MONDAY, JULY 4, 1864: Memorable day

Our forefathers fought seven years for independence, and we have only fought for three. Can we stand it the other four? Yes, we will never give up as long as we can sustain an army, but we hope that long before the end of seven years our enemy will withdraw from our country and leave us in the employment of our liberties under a Government of our own.

The enemy has been very noisy all day celebrating the Fourth, but it brings only remembrances to us. One year ago today we were near Vicksburg, expecting to attack Grant in the rear and relieve the garrison in the beleaguered city, but the brave defenders were at that very moment in the act of capitulating, though we were not informed of it till the morning of the 6th when, with heavy hearts, we began the retreat to Jackson.

TUESDAY, JULY 5, 1864:

"Our friends", the enemy, had a hilarious time last night. They played "Yankee Doodle," "Star Spangled Banner," made speeches, and hurrahed themselves hoarse until late in the night. In fact, we left them at 11 o'clock still enjoying themselves.

We had another all-night march and halted this morning at Chattahoochee River, where we formed line and began throwing up breastworks to protect the railroad bridge. We have had a very quiet time today, scarcely a gun can be heard, except an occasional boom of cannon in the distance. We got another big ration of coffee (65 grains each).

WEDNESDAY, JULY 6, 1864: Chattahoochee River

We have very good ditches ready now but the enemy has not put in an appearance and we enjoy the recess from the popping of guns and the hissing of minie-balls.

THURSDAY, JULY 7, 1864:

The enemy moved up in our front last night and we have had lively skirmishing today. One of our company was severely wounded. In the afternoon we were relieved and moved back in reserve, where we began to fortify, as usual.

FRIDAY, JULY 8, 1864:

Cannonading was heavy last night and we slept in the ditches. At daylight we moved back to the front line and had several skirmishes during the day.

SATURDAY, JULY 9, 1864:

We crossed the Chattahoochee and rested in the woods till afternoon when we began to fortify again. Having the river between the two armies now, what will be the next move? We can't retreat much farther without giving up Atlanta, which certainly will not be done without a desperate struggle, so we may look out for some hard fighting within the next month. Although still largely out-numbered, we hope to be successful and drive Sherman and his hosts back to the Tennessee River.

SUNDAY, JULY 10, 1864: Chattahoochee River, Ga.

After crossing the river last night, we bivouacked in the woods and had a quiet night's rest, as the Chattahoochee was between us and the enemy. But at daylight we were awakened by the burning of the bridge, which the last of our troops set on fire.

During the morning, Sherman moved up on the opposite side and began his usual pastime of shelling the woods. He did not disturb us much as we were safely situated on the southern slope of a high hill, which protected us from the shells. Not so, however, with an old gentleman who lived just in the rear of our line on an elevated place and in range of the shells, which began bursting around him.

Scarcely had the report of the first shell died away, when everything around that home was in confusion: niggers, cattle, horses, and mules, all ready to stampede; but it did not take long for the old man to decide what course to pursue. He was suddenly impressed with the idea that he could not hold his fort and it would be wise to evacuate at once. So, having hitched up his wagon and hastily throwing in a few necessary articles, he began a retreat farther south, followed by the negroes on horseback and mule-back, bareback and astraddle, both men and women.

In the meantime, quite a crowd of us had gone over to see if we could render any assistance, and before leaving the old gentleman said, "Boys, I want you to take everything I leave, for I know the Yankees will get it and I don't want them to eat or drink anything that belongs to me."

We accepted the invitation as hungry soldiers might be expected to do and found large quantities of everything good to eat and drink. Fat hogs in the lot, ham, lard molasses sugar in the pantry, canned goods, preserves, bottled whiskeys and brandies and casks of grape wine in the cellar. This was indeed a feast such as Rebel soldiers had never dreamed of and in striking contrast to our daily fare of cornbread and bacon. We went into it with a relish and the greatest drawback to our happiness was the lack of vessels to carry as much of the liquid refreshments as we desired. However, we got enough and when we returned to the line-of-battle we ate, drank and were "merry."

We remained in line all day and were congratulating ourselves on the prospect of a night's rest when, just at dark, we got orders to "fall in" and moved from one position to another till midnight.

TUESDAY, JULY 12, 1864:

This is the first entire rest day we have had since we left north Alabama ten weeks ago. Nothing to do but lie around in the woods, sleep and eat cornbread and bacon—or at least all who are fortunate to have it.

WEDNESDAY, JULY 13, 1864:

We are still resting undisturbed in the rear. We had preaching and prayer meetings day and night. Many of the boys seem interested in the meetings; we had five conversions at the night meeting.

THURSDAY, JULY 14, 1864:

We moved back into line and the day passed off as so many have since the campaign opened, with picket fighting and an occasional cannonade, with very few casualties on either side.

FRIDAY, JULY 15, 1864:

General Bragg arrived from Richmond. I guess they are getting uneasy about Atlanta and have sent him to see if something can be done to check Sherman's invasion. It is getting to be a serious matter, but we have the utmost confidence in General Johnston and feel like he will devise some plan to hold the city, if we can't whip the Yanks in a fair fight.

SATURDAY, JULY 16, 1864:

Without consulting the officers we have agreed upon an armistice. All firing between pickets has ceased and consequently we have had a very quiet day, with the exception of the artillery, which is not included in the truce.

Johnnies and Yanks have become quite friendly, exchanging many articles, such as tobacco for coffee canteens, etc., but it has to be done on the sly to keep the officers from finding it out as they would hardly sanction so much familiarity.

SUNDAY, JULY 17, 1864:

A pleasant and quiet Sunday. No doubt the officers are wondering why everything is so silent on the picket-line. Of course, we don't propose to volunteer any information, for we are enjoying the respite, and they might have so little regard for our feelings as to break up the truce.

We supplemented our short rations by picking blackberries, of which there is an abundance, every time we get an opportunity. The Christian Association has been reorganized after a lapse of several months and the meetings continue to grow in interest. Part of the command is allowed to attend each service, which is held in the woods by the light of the moon. There is heavy cannonading on the river this evening, probably caused by an attempt of the Yanks to cross.

MONDAY, JULY 18, 1864:

Movements today indicate a fight or a game of "bluff". Troops are hurried from one point to another, lines are drawn closer and our truce is terminated, which is a source of regret. This everlasting sharpshooting is very annoying, while it gives neither side any advantage and cannot hasten the termination of the war.

About 1 p.m. a circular was brought around the lines and read, imparting the sorrowful news that our beloved commander had been removed and General J. B. Hood placed in command. This is a great blow to our cause and has cast a gloom over the whole army. Strong men wept, while others cursed, and not one approved the change.

We think it a terrible mistake of our President. While we believe General Hood to be a brave and efficient officer, capable of commanding a division or even a corps, we doubt his capacity to handle a large army opposed by the wily Sherman with three men to our one. No man in the Confederacy, not even the great Lee himself, could take the place of General Johnston in the confidence and love of the army of Tennessee just at this critical time.

When the first shock had subsided, although there was much discontent and grumbling, duty bade us submit and hope for the best. But many of us still believed it was the worst calamity that could have befallen us and our cause.

TUESDAY, JULY 19, 1864:

Skirmishing has been very brisk all day. Our advance regiment had a sharp engagement, capturing 75 of the enemy. We got a good lot of canteens from the prisoners, swapping tobacco for them.

WEDNESDAY, JULY 20, 1864: Peach Tree Creek, Ga.

The enemy has crossed the Chattahoochee and fortified in our front, while a column is moving around our right flank. Skirmishing was heavy all the morning, and everything indicated that a battle would be fought during the day. We all know that General Hood was placed in command of this army for the express purpose of making a desperate effort to hold Atlanta. While we have not the same confidence in his generalship that we had in General Johnston, we have resolved that if there is a failure, it shall not be our fault.

It is a fearful thing to charge an enemy in his works, especially when outnumbered two or three to one, but feeling that it had to be done we nerved ourselves up to this point to do our whole duty. So when orders came to form in front of the breastworks we were ready. The line being formed, we had to move half a mile or more to the right to fill a gap between us and Hardee's Corps.

This delayed us till 4 o'clock p.m., when we halted and General Stewart made a little speech in which he informed us that we "were going to assault the enemy in his works, and we must carry everything, allowing no obstacle to stop us; that the fate of Atlanta probably depended on the result of this battle."

The order was to charge in echelon, by divisions, at intervals of 200 yards, so when the division on our right had gained the proper distance the command was given, "By the right of companies to the front, march." It was well that such was the order, for we could never have gone through that tangled mass of timber and brush in line-of-battle. It was a heavy-timbered section and the trees had been felled, lapped and crossed until they presented an almost impassable barrier, but we finally made our way through the worst of it and were then halted and wheeled by the left flank into line-of-battle, being then under fire of the pickets.

The order to "fix bayonets, forward, double-quick, march," was given. We raised the old Rebel yell and rushed on the works, but the yell was soon drowned by the roar of musketry and thunder of cannon, canister, and minie-balls mowed great gaps in our ranks, but on we went until it seemed a hand-to-hand conflict was inevitable. Our boys began to waver and soon the line fell back under cover of a little hill, where we reformed our shattered columns and forward again with the same result.

A four gun battery was immediately in our front and the enemy were massed in the ditch. Indeed it seemed like a forlorn hope to attempt to dislodge them, but having rested a short time we made the third charge and drove them from the works, capturing the four cannon, the flag of the 33rd New Jersey, and planting our colors on the breastworks.

We thought the battle was won and were rejoicing over what we supposed would result in a glorious victory, but Hardee's Corps was repulsed on our right and in a short time the Yankees were pouring a galling fire into us from front and flank, which with an enfilading fire of artillery from our right proved so destructive that we were ordered to retire, leaving our captured guns, but holding to the New Jersey flag, which we carried out as a trophy.

Sorrowfully, the survivors retired to our breastworks, mourning the loss of many of our friends, but thankful that we had escaped. Thus General Hood's first battle was a failure, with a loss of probably 4000 or 5000 men, but it was no fault of the troops on our part of the line, for Stewart's corps literally obeyed his orders, carrying everything and with proper support on the right could have driven the enemy across Peach Tree Creek.

Extract from Yankee Official Reports Regarding Battle at Peach Tree Creek

Extract from Official Report of Lt. Col. Enos Fourat, commander, 33rd New Jersey, Serial 73, page 225:

"As the men rose and commenced to retire, with a yell of exultation, the enemy rushed upon us with his dense masses and pressed so close that he ordered the surrender of our colors; with the order we could not comply. The fire was terrific: the air was literally full of deadly missiles, men dropped on all sides; none expected to escape. The bearer of our state colors fell; one of the color guard was killed and one or two missing. The enemy were too close upon us to recover the colors; it was simply impossible and it is with feelings of deepest sorrow I am compelled to report that our state colors fell into the hands of the enemy, at the same time I feel it was no fault of ours. We fought as long as we could. No regiment was more proud of their blue banner than the 33rd New Jersey and none ever fought better to preserve it: it was an impossibility."

Captain Thomas O'Connor of the same regiment says, in part, in his official report, Serial 73, pages 226–231:

"To stand longer was madness, and the order was reluctantly given to retire fighting. The enemy rushed upon us in dense masses, calling to us to surrender our colors. To save the colors was impossible; the state colors fell into the hands of the enemy; in the deepest sorrow we report it."

Battle of Peach Tree Creek

In Serial 74, page 877, General Loring says:

"It was again ordered forward, and the men moved with cold confidence and resolute step in face of the enemy's works and his two lines of battle, when, arriving within 400 or 500 yards of the enemy's works, a terrible fire from his batteries and small arms opened upon us, but the command moved forward with quickened step and a deafening yell, driving the enemy from his position and not stopping until our colors were planted on different points of the breastworks from right to left in a distance of half a mile, and capturing a number of prisoners. On my left, the 35th, 27th, and 49th Alabama regiments, consolidated of Scott's brigade, captured the colors of the 33rd New Jersey regiment and twice captured a 4-gun battery. This brilliant charge of any gallant division was made so rapidly and with such intrepidity that up to this time we had sustained but comparatively small loss. As the enemy fled in confusion from his works the steady aim of the Mississippi, Alabama and Louisiana marksmen of any command produced great slaughter in his ranks."

"This was in the Battle of Peach Tree Creek, Atlanta, Ga., July 20, 1864."

THURSDAY, JULY 21, 1864:

There is no fighting today, except the skirmishers, but we have had a hard day's work strengthening our fortifications, occasionally moving position to the right or left, digging new ditches, only to leave them again for somebody else's benefit. I have not learned our exact loss in yesterday's battle, but the loss in our consolidated regiment is not as heavy as might have been expected, considering the short range at which we fought and the disadvantage we had in making three successive charges on the enemy in his works.

FRIDAY, JULY 22, 1864:

Last night we abandoned our ditches and fell back on Atlanta, forming line-of-battle in the suburbs of the city, where we again began wielding the pick and spade. By daylight we had slight earthworks thrown up, and the enemy moved up and drove in our pickets. We reinforced and drove them back, then they reinforced and drove us back.

This was repeated until half the line-of-battle was on the skirmish-line, and the whole day was spent with charge after charge, amounting at times almost to a regular engagement. It has been a lively day with all, for those who were not on the skirmish line were throwing dirt with all their might, and by night we had pretty fair works and felt like we could hold our position against any attack.

General Hardee's corps attacked the Federal left at about 2 p.m., but we took no part except as interested listeners. The battle raged furiously for three hours and although our troops captured three lines of works, quite a number of prisoners and artillery, there was no decisive advantage gained and Hardee moved back to his old line. Now the Gate City is invested, and no doubt Sherman will attempt another flank movement.

SATURDAY, JULY 23, 1864:

I learned this morning that Major General McPherson, of the Federal army, and Maj. Gen. Walker, of the Confederate army were killed in yesterday's battle.

Last night, about dusk, Sherman opened his batteries on the city. All night long shells and solid shot passed over our heads and went crashing through residences.

Some of the boys raided a potato patch, and today got us a good mess of Irish potatoes, which we enjoyed very much for dinner. The patch was between the line and very near the enemy, but by crawling down the rows, keeping heads below the potato tops, they succeeded in "grabbing" a good lot without being discovered.

General Stewart issued a circular urging us "to stand by our glorious cause through weal and woe, to work night and day to strengthen our fortifications so a few men can hold them while the rest operate on the flanks; that this is the place and the time has come when we must make a grand struggle for our independence, and that the operations of the next few days may go a great way towards deciding the fate of the Confederacy."

MONDAY, JULY 25, 1864:

The enemy continues the war upon women and children, the shelling having been kept up almost uninterruptedly since Saturday, occasionally dropping a few among us by way of diversion. Our batteries have replied at intervals only, not having ammunition to waste.

Our regiment is now supporting a battery of siege guns which has been thundering away for three or four hours, and just at night we sent a large shell which busted among the commissary wagons, causing a stampede. I never heard such a racket—teams running, camp kettles and cooking utensils rattling, and drivers yelling, "whoa!, whoa!, whoa!."

Of course, we enjoyed it, and the Yanks hearing us laughing over it, said it was a "blank" shame to shoot right into their commissary wagons before they got their supper, and they would get even with us before the campaign was over.

TUESDAY, JULY 26, 1864: Atlanta, Ga.

We were relieved last night by "Governor Brown's Pets" (Georgia State Troops) and sent back to the rear to rest, which we needed very much.

WEDNESDAY, JULY 27, 1864:

We are still resting, but it has rained on us most of the day. Cannonading and skirmishing has been quite heavy. Brigadier General Ector was killed by a shell.

THURSDAY, JULY 28, 1864:

Another memorable day to us. Having had a good rest of 36 hours, we were ordered to fall in and took the Newman road. Lee's corps has been skirmishing all the morning, and as we moved in that direction, we surmised correctly that the boys were needing help.

By 12 o'clock the battle had fairly begun and we changed from a quick to a double quick, reaching the battleground at 1 p.m. We had run about four miles and were quite out of breath, but they didn't give us time to "blow." We were rushed right in where the bullets were coming thick as hail and having no breast-works on either side it was a fair open field fight.

We charged them and they charged us. Neither side yielded much and the battle raged, stubbornly contested, until night put an end to the conflict, and we held the field, but that was all the advantage we could claim.

Our division remained all night on the battlefield, and my company was placed near where most of the dead and wounded lay, where we sat all night long, watching for the enemy and listening to the groans of the wounded and dying, not allowed to sleep and could not sleep if we were allowed, passing a horrible night.

Since General Hood took command (within the past eight days) we have fought three battles with a loss of at least 10,000 men and have gained nothing, so far as I am able to see. No doubt the enemy's loss has been as great as ours, but we cannot afford to swap man for man, for if it is kept up we will soon be wiped out, leaving Sherman with a large army and none to oppose him. Generals Stewart and Loring are both among the wounded of today's battle.

FRIDAY, JULY 29, 1864: Near Atlanta, Ga.

At daybreak we withdrew from the battlefield, falling back one mile, where we began, as usual, with pick and spade, taking it by turns; some slept while others worked as we were almost exhausted from the fatigue of yesterday and the long, silent watch all night. If we accomplished nothing else we got a good din-ner as the result of yesterday's battle. When the battle closed, our line ran through a farmyard where there were quite a lot of chickens, and my mess had the good fortune to capture several nice frying size, which we held prisoner till today, when we fried them for dinner and enjoyed it immensely.

SATURDAY, JULY 30, 1864:

We worked by detail all yesterday and last night and this morning feel that we are prepared for Mr. Sherman, although we are stretched out in a single rank, which we have to do to cover his front, his line being so much longer than ours. He keeps moving around our left and we have to lengthen our line correspondingly.

We are now three or four miles west of Atlanta, and have been very quiet since the 28th, but there is heavy cannonading around the city and no doubt the pickets will begin to close up on us soon.

SUNDAY, JULY 31, 1864:

Our regiment went on picket last night, but as the enemy was not very near, we had nothing to do but sit still and watch. Maj. Gen. Cheatam now commands our corps temporarily.

MONDAY, AUGUST 1, 1864: Near East Point, Ga.

General Roddy arrived yesterday with his brigade dismounted for the emer-gency. He got to East Point just in time to capture a raiding party of Yankees and recapture some of our boys who were prisoners. In the afternoon our brigade moved three miles to the right, which places us near the city again.

WEDNESDAY, AUGUST 3, 1864:

Sherman is still shelling the city and heavy skirmishing all along the line as far as the sound of the guns can reach us. Bullets from the skirmishers are flying around promiscuously, making it dangerous to be above ground, but we have long since learned to take care of No. 1 and keep closely covered in our ditches.

THURSDAY, AUG. 4–THURSDAY, AUG. 11, 1864: Atlanta

During the past eight days no engagement worthy of being called a battle has been fought. The usual skirmishing and cannonading has been going on, sometimes enlivened by a charge of the pickets from one side or the other. We have moved position several times, but the night of the 11th finds us occupying our old ditches in the western suburbs of the city and the enemy fortified about three hundred yards in our front.

FRIDAY, AUGUST 12, 1864:

The enemy is moving large forces to our left, no doubt endeavoring to swing around our rear and cut the railroads on which we depend for supplies. Our brigade was today detached and sent to East Point, six miles southwest of the city, and attached to Cleburne's division, making us the extreme left of the army. As soon as we got our line established, picks and spades were brought out and all went to work, as usual.

SATURDAY, AUGUST 13, 1864:

The Yanks are still moving large forces to our left, but have not closed in on us yet; consequently, we are having a very quiet time. We can hear the skirmishing on different parts of the line and the shelling of the city has been continuous and heavy all night and day.

SUNDAY, AUGUST 14, 1864:

We were ordered back and took position west of the city near the place we left a few days ago. We had a heavy rain, which cooled the atmosphere and gave us a good soaking.

MONDAY, AUGUST 15, 1864:

We moved down on the railroad and went to work on the second line of fortifications. Here we are not annoyed by sharpshooters and enjoy a good deal more freedom, not being confined to the ditches like we have been most of the time. Only an occasional shell causes us to seek cover, but as soon as the scare is over we are out again.

TUESDAY, AUGUST 16, 1864:

We have been ordered to East Point again and rejoined Cleburne's division, now on the extreme left again, but no enemy in sight.

WEDNESDAY, AUGUST 17, 1864:

This has been one of the most quiet days of this long and weary campaign on our part of the line. The Yanks have not advanced in our front and we have nothing to do but lie around and listen to the booming of the guns near the city. When the force which has been moving in this direction will turn up we do not know, but no doubt we will hear from them before long.

THURSDAY, AUGUST 18, 1864:

The Chaplains, having taken advantage of our resting spell, had a rousing meeting last night resulting in several accessions to the Christian Association and 40 mourners.

FRIDAY, AUGUST 19, 1864:

Our cavalry has been driven in and the enemy is advancing. A large force of Federal cavalry passed our left and cut both railroads. Our brigade was ordered forward and entirely detached from the main line to take the place of the cavalry that is following the raiding party. We are "web-foot" cavalry now sure enough and may look out for lively times, unless all signs fail.

SATURDAY, AUGUST 20, 1864:

Our cavalry are still after the raiders and we are doing the scouting on foot. The enemy having disappeared from our front, our regiment was ordered on a scout to find them, and before we got back we would have been glad if we hadn't found them. We went about four or five miles through thickets and fields, and on emerging from a large cornfield we ran right into a column of Yankees before we knew it.

It looked like Sherman's whole army must be marching down that road. They seemed somewhat surprised, and not knowing our strength, acted very cautiously, deploying skirmishers parallel with their line, opened fire on us, which we returned and it was only a few minutes before we were in a mighty hot place.

We were holding our own pretty well, under the circumstances, when looking to the right we saw a great cloud of dust rising and, there being nothing to obstruct the view, soon discerned it was a body of the enemy (apparently about a brigade) going in a double-quick to our rear. They were a full half mile from us and we should have about the same distance to run to pass the point they were making for, so the Colonel, thinking "discretion the better part of valor," ordered a retreat.

The Yanks behind us gave a yell and a parting shot which spurred us on, and we went through that field like a hurricane. It was "nip and tuck" and only a question of speed and endurance who should get there first, but we sustained our reputation as cavalry remarkably well and covered that half mile in about as short a space of time as Wheeler's best mounted regiment could have done it. It was an exciting race and with the advantage we had of empty haversacks and no incumbrance of baggage, we just did win by a close shave.

Having successfully run the gauntlet and reached a place of safety, we rested a short time and then proceeded to hunt up the brigade, which we found just ready to start on a scout about six miles down the railroad, where it was reported the enemy were tearing up the track. Although very tired from our tramp of eight or ten miles we fell in with them and made a rapid march to the place where we found about one hundred yards of the track torn up, but the Yanks were gone.

We retraced our steps through the mud and the rain that had been falling for the past two hours, reaching our position at dusk, when we expected to get a little rest. In this we were disappointed, for our regiment was immediately ordered out on picket and we were about as mad a set as was ever seen.

SUNDAY, AUGUST 21, 1864:

We had a long, dreary, rainy night; stood on picket all night without a wink of sleep and we are feeling considerable used up from our hard service yesterday and want of sleep last night. In the afternoon we came back to our old place on the extreme left of the line.

MONDAY, AUGUST 22, 1864:

Our cavalry pressed Kilpatrick so closely that he had to retire to the rear of the Federal army, doing but little damage on his raid. Our cavalry has returned and relieved us for which we are truly thankful, as acting cavalry "on foot" is a new branch of the service and one which we do not relish. If they would furnish us with good horses, we would not object to the change.

We moved one mile to the right and had to go on picket again, and all the troops in our rear have moved, we know not where, leaving only our thin skirmish-line, with no support to fall back on if the enemy should advance.

TUESDAY, AUGUST 23, 1864:

Our situation is unchanged. No Yankees are near enough to bother us, but we are in bad shape to resist them if they only knew it. Cannonading and skirmishing is heavy on the right.

WEDNESDAY, AUGUST 24, 1864:

We are still on the picket line with no support behind us and our regiment moved to the front and deployed by twos 20 paces apart. We are now near the enemy and the sharpshooters are annoying us. We are furnished with tools and each couple is hard at work digging a rifle-pit to protect us from them and the stray bullets of the pickets.

THURSDAY, AUGUST 25, 1864: On the left, near East Point, Ga.

What's the matter on the other side today? The Yanks are making such a terrible racket. It seems as if all the bands and drums in Sherman's army are concentrated in our front and all playing at the same time. Evidently, they are up to some trick, but noise don't scare half as bad as bullets.

If they only knew that we have nothing but a thin picket line in front of them they could have an easy thing, but I hope they won't find it out till we get some support to fall back on.

FRIDAY, AUGUST 26, 1864:

The enemy either got disgusted with their noise or concluded they had accomplished their objective and quieted down about night, leaving us undisturbed. We got some sleep, having two to a pit; one slept while the other watched, and when daylight came peace seemed to reign over both armies from one end of the line to the other. Even the artillery has ceased firing and we have nothing to do but sit in our pits and conjecture what will be next on the program. It is reported that Sherman has withdrawn from the front of Atlanta and we surmise that something will happen on the left in a short time.

SATURDAY, AUGUST 27, 1864:

We had another half-night's sleep, taking it by turns as we did the night before, and the question asked, but not answered, this morning was, "What has become of the Yanks?" Not a drum, or a bugle could be heard, the pickets were all idle and everything as quiet as Sunday but in the afternoon we were ordered out on a scout and we found out where some of the Yanks were at least.

We had gone something near a mile without seeing anything blue, when suddenly we ran right into a column that was moving to our left. They opened fire on us and we skedaddled. We made for cover as fast as our legs could carry us, regardless of range. We succeeded in getting out of the scrape with whole skins, barring a few scratches from briars and limbs.

SUNDAY, AUGUST 28, 1864:

We learned that the column which we encountered yesterday has struck the W. P. & A. Railroad five miles below East Point, and another is moving towards the M. & A. in our rear. Troops are hurrying down there and a battle may be expected.

MONDAY, AUGUST 29, 1864:

The movement of the Feds continues around our left and rear. We will have to fight or evacuate very soon. We left our rifle-pits and marched five miles to the left to a new line and began fortifying.

TUESDAY, AUGUST 30, 1864:

A battle will be fought somewhere below Atlanta within 18 hours. The bulk of the Federal army has swung around and, if not already in possession, will soon have two of our most important railroads. Unless we can drive them back we will be compelled to evacuate.

WEDNESDAY, AUGUST 31, 1864:

Just at dusk last evening we received orders to go to Jonesboro with all possible haste and had a hard, tiresome march all night, reaching the vicinity of Jonesboro before daylight, when our brigade was immediately ordered back to rejoin our division. We have been attached to Cleburne's division for the past two or three weeks.

Although very tired and footsore, we were more than willing to go back for all signs indicated that Jonesboro would be a very unhealthy place before the setting of the sun. And so it proved to be. Before we had covered half the distance the booming of cannon told us that the life or death struggle for Atlanta had begun, and while our sympathies were with the boys who were bearing the brunt of the battle, we rejoiced that it was our good fortune to escape the terrible ordeal.

We got back to our division about midnight, broken down, almost starved, and no rations in sight. Here everything was quiet, and we had nothing to do but sit and listen with intense interest to the thunder of artillery and roar of musketry, which began about 2 p.m. and continued without intermission until darkness put an end to the conflict, our suspense still unrelieved, for we could hear nothing authentic from the battlefield.

All the sick and disabled are ordered to the division hospital. Lt. C., who has been quite sick several days, was so exhausted by the march last night that he had to go, much against his will.

SATURDAY, SEPTEMBER 3, 1864: Atlanta, Ga.

With the dawn of September 1st, the artillery opened again at Jonesboro with what we supposed was a continuation of the battle. All day we listened, our suspense being even greater than it was the day before. Hoping for the best, but no tidings of encouragement reached us, and not until sunset did we learn the true state of affairs. When the news was imparted to us it was a death knell to our hopes.

Our forces were defeated yesterday, and all the firing of today was by artillery to keep up a show of resistance while preparations were being made to evacuate the city. When darkness set in the artillery and wagons began moving, siege guns were spiked and dismounted. Government stores, ammunition and everything that could not be carried out were set on fire. About 10 o'clock, with "heavy hearts and solemn tread," we marched through the city and out in a southeast direction. We traveled all night and at daybreak could see the lights from the fires in the city. Daylight brought no rest; on, on, on all day and all night again we dragged our weary limbs and reached Lovejoy Station on September 3rd. We have been two days and nights without sleep or rest, except a few short stops.

No doubt Sherman thought he had us "bagged" this time, but by taking a very circuitous route, passing around the Federal army, which is still at Jonesboro, we reached our destination without any serious mishap.

SUNDAY, SEPTEMBER 4, 1864: Lovejoy Station, Ga.

We have spent the past three days resting, washing and cleaning up generally. The first wash day we have had for four months and the first regular camp we have enjoyed for some time.

The campaign seems to have ended for the present, but how soon another will begin is more than we can tell, though probably as soon as both armies have time to rest and reorganize. This has been a remarkable campaign. Four long months we've been in line-of-battle. Scarcely one hour during that time, day and night, have we been out of the sound of guns on some part of the line. We have spent many sleepless nights on picket, on vidette or on the retreat. We have dug 100 miles or more of ditches, retreated from Dalton to Atlanta, and now from Atlanta to Lovejoy. We have fought many battles, in nearly all of which the advantage has been on our side, until the fatal 18th of July, when General Hood superseded our beloved commander. Since that time it has been a series of defeats that have left our army shattered and reduced in numbers, but not as much dispirited as might have been expected.

In the four principal battles fought by General Hood, viz, 20th, 22nd and 28th of July and the 31st of August, the tactics of General Johnston were reversed and we had to charge works manned by largely superior numbers and while we feel that we did our whole duty, we were defeated in each, with an aggregate loss of 12,000 to 15,000 men.

Although Gen. Johnston would probably have given up Atlanta, we believe he would have held it longer with much smaller loss and inflicted a heavier loss upon the enemy. Our army would now be stronger and in better condition, but we do not censure General Hood, for he is a brave and gallant officer and was placed in command for the express purpose of making a desperate struggle to hold the "Gate City."

However, it is evident now, as we then believed, that President Davis made a fatal mistake when he issued the order relieving General Johnston.

THURSDAY, SEPTEMBER 8, 1864:

We have been ordered to call roll three times a day. Company drills in the morning and battalion drills in the afternoon. We learned that the Chicago Convention nominated McClellan and Pendleton for President and Vice-President.

SATURDAY, SEPTEMBER 10, 1864:

An armistice for 10 days has been agreed upon by the commanding Generals to be effective within five miles of the railroad. Outside of that territory operation can be carried on as usual. Sherman has ordered every white person out of Atlanta.

What are the poor people to do? Forty thousand or 50,000 have been driven from their homes, upon an already impoverished country, leaving all behind, without money, food or shelter. It is distressing, cruel and I can't believe it would have been done if things were reversed and we had captured a Northern city. But, such is war, and stimulates us to a renewed determination to achieve our independence or die in the last ditch.

SUNDAY, SEPTEMBER 11, 1864:

Preaching services were held between the hours of duty today. An attempt is being made to renew the revival that has been interrupted for so long a time.

MONDAY, SEPTEMBER 12, 1864:

Nothing of interest going on except the "big meeting." Twenty-five were baptized today.

TUESDAY, SEPTEMBER 13, 1864:

Interest in the revival grows. Twenty more were baptized and many penitents at the altar. Preaching and drilling takes up about all our time.

WEDNESDAY, SEPTEMBER 14, 1864:

Division review today. General Loring mounted on his old roan, rode down the line, welcomed by cheers from the whole division. He had just returned, having been wounded on July 28th.

THURSDAY, SEPTEMBER 15, 1864:

Governor Brown of Georgia has appointed this a day of fasting and prayer, and requests the Army of Tennessee to observe it. We have been fasting most of the time for two years, but I am afraid not enough prayers are associated with the "fast" to avail much.

FRIDAY, SEPTEMBER 16, 1864:

Our corps was reviewed today by General Hood, about 8000 in line. The revival continues with unabated interest. Everybody is trying to get religion. Let the good work go on, for they certainly need it.

Sherman is enforcing his order expelling the white people from Atlanta. Federal army wagons bring the refugees to Rough and Ready, where ours meet and carry them beyond our lines.

SATURDAY, SEPT. 17 TO SATURDAY NOV. 26, 1864:

Our truce expired on the 21st and it was soon apparent that active operations would be resumed in a short time, of course, being ignorant of what the movement would be. Of one thing we were certain, that we were in no condition to meet Sherman in the open field, and that it must be another retreat or an attempt to get in his rear, cut off his supplies and force him back to the Tennessee River.

President Davis visited us on the 25th, and the next day inspected the army. When riding along the lines many of the men called out loudly, "Give us Johnston," or, "Send General Johnston back and we will whip Sherman yet," and many similar remarks to which the President made no reply.

On the 28th we were formed in line and not until the head of the column started northward did we know what direction we would take. We crossed the Chattahoochee River on the 29th and our corps was detached from the main army, Loring's division striking the railroad at Acworth, where we captured a blockhouse with 250 prisoners.

French's division attacked Allatoona and after a desperate battle was repulsed by the garrison under General Corse. We then followed the railroad, tearing up many miles of track, demolishing cars, and destroying everything which could be of any use to the Federal army.

On the 10th of October we passed through the battlefield of New Hope Church. This battle was fought on the 25th of May, when the trees were in full leaf, and by getting on an elevated place we could see the line-of-battle stretching out for miles, and trace the exact position of the two armies by deadened timber from one-quarter to half-mile in width.

I had often heard it remarked as being strange that so few men were killed in battle, considering the number of shots fired, but here was a visible solution of the mystery. The trees between the lines were literally torn to pieces on both sides and, while quite a number of bullets struck as low as a man's head, a large majority of them ranged from 10, 20 and 30 feet from the ground, proving that most of us, under the excitement, aimed too high.

On October 11, Sherman crossed the Chattahoochee with 65,000 men and followed on our trail, but General Hood, being unwilling to risk a battle, kept moving on and after a chase of several days Sherman gave it up, returned to Atlanta and shortly afterwards started on his memorable "March to the Sea."

We reached Dalton on the 13th, where we captured 1000 prisoners, 800 of whom were negroes, and these men were the last Federal troops we saw until we arrived at Decatur, Alabama.

From Dalton we turned in a southwesterly direction and marched to Gadsden, Alabama where General Beauregard met us and a consultation was held to decide whether we should follow Sherman (as he wouldn't follow us) or go on into Tennessee. It was finally decided to go on and leave the enemy unmolested in their march through Georgia. It was rather an unusual thing for two opposing armies to be going as fast as they could in opposite directions.

Accordingly, the head of our column was turned northward again and after a few days of hard marching through Sand Mountain, we struck the Tennessee Valley above Decatur, then down the Valley and at Decatur found a garrison strongly fortified. We expected to have to storm the works, but I presume General Hood thought it not of sufficient importance to justify the loss it would necessarily entail to take the place.

General Hood intended to cross the Tennessee at or above Decatur, but by this time rations, which had been short ever since we left Lovejoy, had about given out and we were unable to get subsistence from the country. So we turned down the river and reached Tuscumbia the latter part of October, where we went into camps.

The portion of the regiment who lived in adjacent counties were given passes for 48 hours to visit home. We remained at Tuscumbia three weeks, expecting orders every day to cross the river and begin the march into Tennessee. We became very restless knowing that every day's delay gave the enemy opportunity to concentrate forces to oppose us. But the railroad from Corinth had not been repaired as ordered by General Hood, consequently all supplies had to be hauled in wagons from Cherokee, 16 miles distant. The roads were almost impassable and much valuable time was consumed in getting sufficient supplies for the trip into Tennessee.

On November 19, 1864, Forrest's Cavalry crossed the river. General Buford said he could not pass without seeing his old brigade and it was equally pleasant for us to greet him again. After a general hand-shaking, he made a little speech in which he said, in part, he "would like to have us with him if we were mounted, but as that could not be he knew we would do our duty wherever placed, and it was not by the dash of the cavalry, but by the heavy blows of the infantry that we might expect to achieve our independence."

We crossed on November 20th and the march without unusual incident except that quite a number of stragglers were killed by bushwhackers in the hills of Wayne County. It was said they were mutilated beyond recognition, of this I have no positive knowledge, but there is no doubt that they were shot from ambush at every opportunity.

General Forrest drove the small forces of the enemy before him, so we did not come in contact with them until we reached the vicinity of Columbia on the morning of November 28th.

SUNDAY, NOVEMBER 27, 1864:

The frequent stops of the column, the dashing about of staff officers and couriers indicated early in the day that there was some obstruction ahead, and we surmised correctly that the Yanks were not far off.

When within four miles of Columbia our corps filed to the right. After winding about through fields and woods and over small country roads we struck the Pulaski pike. Here our regiment was deployed as skirmishers, and advanced in line till it encountered the enemy's pickets, when it was halted and ordered to "rest on arms."

MONDAY, NOVEMBER 28, 1864:

We rested very well, some sleeping while others watched, till 2 a.m. when we were roused and ordered forward, feeling our way through the darkness, expecting every moment to be fired into, but it wasn't long before the luminous fires and vivid flashes of burning ammunition indicated that the enemy had evacuated. Still we advanced slowly and cautiously, entering the town just at daybreak.

We were met by citizens of both sexes, who grasped our hands and with tears of joy bid us welcome, so glad to see the Rebels once more. They brought us hot coffee, biscuits, and everything good to eat and how we enjoyed it. Our regiment was made provost-guard and we had a royal time all day. The citizens furnishing us cooked rations of the very best they had, and filling our haversacks to overflowing.

The enemy, after crossing the river formed line-of-battle on the north bank. When our forces came up a sharp little fight occurred that we witnessed, but took no part in, though stray bullets frequently struck uncomfortably near us, causing us to dodge behind houses for shelter.

After the skirmish we began gathering up the commissary stores and other plunder that the Yankees had failed to burn. This kept us busy a good part of the day, but when we were not at work, the younger portion of us were engaged in the more agreeable business of talking to the pretty young women.

TUESDAY, NOVEMBER 29, 1864:

This morning we found the enemy still occupying the north bank of the river, so we moved six miles above, crossed and began a race to get in their rear. General Hood issues a circular stating that his "intention was to beat them to Nashville, that he expects us to march hard and not give up under any circumstances."

When we reached the crossing place, our cavalry had opened the way and having nothing to oppose us, we went forward with high hopes of intercepting the force that we left at Columbia.

After a hard day's march we arrived at Spring Hill at dusk, in advance of quite a body of the enemy, and expected to dispute their passage. Instead, we were allowed to bivouac parallel with and only a short distance from the road, where we could hear them passing all night.

Having accomplished the very thing which General Hood asked us to, it was provoking to have to lie still and let the golden opportunity slip away from us, without even an attempt to reap the fruit of our forced march, which seemed to be within our grasp. Every private was impressed with the idea that a fearful blunder had been made, and many remarks were made uncomplimentary to those in command. Of course, we were not in a position to know who was responsible for the failure.

WEDNESDAY, NOVEMBER 30, 1864:

We were awakened before daylight and our mortification was even greater than it was last night to find that the game had flown; every last one of them had "walked right out of the trap" and was hurrying on towards Franklin.

We were ordered to fall in promptly and were soon strung out in hot pursuit, pressing them so closely during the day that they were forced to burn about 50 wagons, the smoldering remains of which were scattered along the road for several miles. But no doubt they were rejoicing at their easy escape from a very perilous position. Judging from the way they traveled, they did not intend to allow us to get them into a similar scrape today.

Four miles from Franklin, they formed line across the road as if they were going to make a stand, but this was intended only to gain time and delay us. As soon as our brigade, which was in front, formed line-of-battle, they withdrew and continued their retreat.

In order to avoid similar delays, we were marched by the right of battalions to the front, keeping up our line so that in case of necessity we could wheel into line-of-battle on short notice. However, they did not make any further show of fight and we continued the march through wood and fields, until we reached the line of hills about two miles south of Franklin.

Here, while waiting for the rest of the command to come up, we had a good view of the town. The intervening space being almost level, with not a tree to obstruct the view, we could see the enemy's wagons hurrying across the little river and the Yankees themselves in two or three lines throwing up earthworks with the greatest activity.

They were evidently preparing to give us a warm reception, which afterwards proved to be about the warmest we had ever met.

When the remainder of the army arrived and were taking their places in line, our division (Loring's) was ordered to move by the right flank. We had gone but a short distance when we encountered the enemy's cavalry. Wheeling into line we drove them into the timber above the town. Our cavalry continued skirmishing, but failed to move them any farther. About 3 p.m. our brigade was ordered to the cavalry's assistance and with a yell we charged and then drove them half a mile farther up the river.

While we were driving the cavalry, the remainder of the army including Adam's and Featherstone's brigades of our division formed immediately in front of the town on both sides of the Columbia pike and moved forward in two and three lines. Level fields stretched out in front of the enemy and it was a fearful ordeal to charge a fortified position under such disadvantages. When we emerged from the timber we saw our men within 300 yards of the works advancing through the open fields under the most destructive fire we ever witnessed. Although great gaps were being cut in their ranks they moved steadily forward and drove the enemy from the first-line, then on to the second where a most deadly conflict took place with nothing between them except the embankment the Federals had thrown up for protection of their infantry.

We were entirely detached from our main columns but a left wheel brought us into line facing the upper part of the town, the right of our brigade resting on Harpeth River. General Scott galloped down the line urging us to "hurry up: that the enemy were retreating and General Hood wanted us to charge and capture them before they could cross the river." The enemy had several batteries on a range of hills just across the little river which fired over their own lines until the opposing forces got so close together they endangered their own men. Then they concentrated all the guns on us, being on the extreme right and nearest to them with nothing but open space between. Our position threw us in direct line with the batteries on the hill which enfilades us every shot, but we pressed forward and when near enough the infantry opened on us with terrible volleys and it seemed as if not one of us could escape the storm of shells, canister and bullets which were poured into us. Our troops who were massed further to our left had failed to make a breach in the works and before we could reach the works our single line had become so thinned and nearly every officer killed or disabled. With none to command or lead it would have simply resulted in a massacre for us to proceed further. We had reached the railroad cut and took such cover as that afforded and in the abandoned rifle pits of the enemy where we were partially protected and remained till darkness set in.

On the Columbia pike the battle continued to rage with fury. The Confederates had got to the works, but their ranks were so thinned it was impossible to dislodge the enemy who were massed in the ditch. They could neither advance nor retreat and in almost a hand to hand conflict, the dreadful work of carnage was kept up till midnight when the enemy silently withdrew and evacuated the town.*

The next morning a sad scene met our eyes when it was light enough to see. Our dead were literally piled on top of each other at the foot of the embankment that alone separated them from the dead Federals in the ditch on the opposite side. Dead and wounded were scattered for hundreds of yards in front of the works. The percentage of loss was equal to, or perhaps greater than, any battle of the war considering the number engaged and the duration of the battle.

The loss in our brigade was quite heavy, but we suffered less than those who bore the brunt of the battle on the Columbia pike. Of our regiment, Major Dixon was killed and Colonel Ives received several very bad wounds which were thought to be mortal, but he finally recovered after months of suffering. Colonel John D. Weeden of 49th Alabama commanded the consolidated regiment from that time to the close of the war.

---

* In Serial 93, page 708, General A. P. Stewart, commanding the corps, says in his report, "The men, however, pressed forward again and again, with dauntless courage, to the ditch around the inner line of works which they failed to carry, but where many of them remained, separated from the enemy only by the parapet, until the Federal Army withdrew." Ed.

This was a dearly bought victory, if victory it was, and nothing accomplished that could not have been done without the loss of a man: for the Federals were evidently forced to fight against their will and would have evacuated during the night. We spent the day burying the dead and taking care of the wounded as best we could and late in the afternoon crossed the river and started on the march to Nashville.

As my diary gives a detailed account of our operations around Nashville, I quote from it again.

FRIDAY, DECEMBER 2, 1864:

Early this morning we got into line and marched briskly until 2 p.m., when we file to the left and after maneuvering about in the night until we were about five or six miles from the city of Nashville.

SATURDAY, DECEMBER 3, 1864:

We remained quietly in line till 2 p.m., when we were ordered forward in line-of-battle, charged the enemy's skirmishers and drove them back, advancing in sight of the enemy's works, and were ordered to lie down. Being in plain view of their line, the artillery opened on us and gave us a severe shelling, during which quite a number were killed and wounded. After a while getting so destructive we were ordered under cover of a hill, where we remained till night, when we moved a short distance to the left and began fortifying.

SUNDAY, DECEMBER 4, 1864:

We worked hard all night, believing that the shelling would be renewed with daylight and that our safety depended in large measure on the depths into which we succeeded getting into the ground. Sure enough, as soon as it was light enough to see, "the dogs of war" were let loose again and a terrific shelling was kept up all day with but little damage to us, as we were pretty well sheltered by our breastworks. The only serious casualty in our regiment being that of Jack Nichols, who was mortally wounded by a fragment of shell.

The enemy have a strong position, their artillery being posted on commanding eminences, with nothing but open fields between us, while a line of earthworks for the infantry extends as far as we can see. If we are to storm their works, it seems to me it should be done at once as every hour's delay is adding to their strength and no advantage to us.

FRIDAY, DECEMBER 9, 1864:

It is very cold and snowing. We moved back to the breastworks.

SUNDAY, DECEMBER 11, 1864:

Last night, under cover of darkness, we moved our line back 400 yards and began fortifying again. We worked hard all night without sleep or rest. This is the coldest day I ever saw. Our position being in the open fields, with no timber for miles to break the force of the wind, which is blowing a perfect gale from the north, no wood to make fires and most of us thinly clad, our suffering is intense. It seems like we are bound to freeze unless a change occurs very soon.

TUESDAY, DECEMBER 13, 1864:

The enemy, no doubt, have been largely reinforced, and are extending their lines beyond our flanks, rendering it necessary for us to lengthen our lines; but having all our available force already in the ditches, we can only do it by forming a single rank. This causes a change in location and, as usual, it falls to our lot to stop where there are no works, so we have again to call into requisition our old friends, the pick and the spade.

It is discouraging to leave our quarters so often, after such hard work digging ditches to protect us from shells and cold winds. But we go to work again, and every bomb and bullet that comes by only stresses to renew our energy. In a short time we have a new ditch, as good as the old one.

WEDNESDAY, DECEMBER 14, 1864:

The weather has moderated, and we enjoy lying around in the sun, but the Yanks won't let us enjoy it for any length of time. When they see a squad of us, they drop over a few shells and we dart into holes like prairie dogs.

We are still stretched out in a single rank, a very weak line, but with the advantage of our breastworks, have confidence in our ability to hold our position against any ordinary attack.

THURSDAY, DECEMBER 15, 1864:

A heavy fog overhung the city and all the surrounding country this morning, so we could see nothing that was going on in front. The Yanks took advantage of it in disposing their forces for an attack on our lines.

At 10 a.m. they opened with a furious shelling, drove in our pickets, and took possession of the works we abandoned a few days ago. Our artillery replied with vigor, and a fearful cannonade was soon in progress all around the line, which continued without intermission for several hours.

Now and then, the infantry moved forward as if they were going to assault our works, but a few rounds from us drove them back in every instance.

About 2 p.m very heavy fighting could be heard on the left and, as the sound of the guns receded, it soon became evident they had turned our left wing. We still hoped that our boys would rally and regain what had been lost, believing that we could hold our position. This we subsequently proved, for in a short time they moved forward in heavy columns and made two determined assaults that we repulsed.

We were now too busily engaged to observe what was going on to our left. During a lull in the battle, to our dismay, we found that everything to the left of our division had given way and the Federals had swung around and were sweeping down our line not more than two hundred yards distant.

Those in front, encouraged by the success of their right wing, made another furious onslaught, and the flanking column bearing down upon us at the same time. Our weak line of one rank could not stand the pressure and it was only a question of retreat or surrender and quite a number of our regiment surrendered on the spot.

The remainder of us struck out diagonally to the rear in order to avoid both lines as much as possible. We fell back in considerable disorder for something near half a mile. We rallied and opened on them with the effect of checking their advance.

We remained on this line till dark, when we moved back one mile and formed line-of-battle, our position being behind a stone fence and still in one rank. Here we made such preparations as we could to get a little rest and be ready for the stirring times that we are sure will come tomorrow.

FRIDAY, DECEMBER 16, 1864:

At daylight the booming of cannon all along the line awakened those of us who were inclined to slumber and foretokened the dreadful ordeal through which we were to pass today. It is seldom the case that an army is in worse condition for meeting its enemy in "battle's dread array" than ours is at this time. Having suffered numerous defeats in the past six months by an overwhelming force, only yesterday driven from our works, thousands killed and captured, we are now reduced to less than 20,000 effectives. Opposed by a victorious army numbering perhaps more than two to one, it was to be expected they would come with redoubled energy today.

Realizing all these disadvantages, we could but feel somewhat dispirited. With a determination to do our whole duty, we nerved ourselves up to the point of making one more heroic effort to stay the tide of disaster that has befallen us. We awaited the attack with the deepest solicitude.

As soon as the sun had dispelled the morning mists we could see two lines of blue drawn up before us, while the artillery from its commanding position was dealing death and destruction in our thinned ranks.

The cannonading was terrific and continued almost without intermission during the day. Shells and solid shot passed through the stone fence behind which we were sheltered, scattering stones in every direction and mangling men in a shocking manner.

To lie still under such a destructive artillery fire produces a feeling of dread that cannot be described. This is more demoralizing than to be actively engaged in battle; but we had to endure it for six long hours without even a skirmish to divert our attention.

Our artillery replied only occasionally, husbanding their ammunition, which was scarce, for the final contest they all knew must come before long. About 1 o'clock p.m. the enemy made an attack on our left, gradually driving our boys back until the fighting seemed to be almost in our rear. Then "hurrah, hurrah, hurrah" was heard in our front and we knew the "tug of war" was coming.

All dread vanished and excitement took its place. On they came, two lines of blue, through the open field, in a double quick. Our old reliable pointe coupee (our brigade battery) opened at once, first with shell and, as they approached nearer, with grape canister. Then a storm of minie-balls was let loose from behind the stone fence, and the yells of Confederates and "hurrah" of Yankees were drowned under the roar of musketry and artillery. Men were falling on both sides and it seemed for a time that the bayonet would be the means of ending the contest. A few more rounds made it so hot that the enemy began retiring, though only for a short distance. Rallying, they moved forward again, and the battle raged fiercer than before.

Still confident that we could hold our position, we defiantly called to them to come on, but they seemed unwilling to come to close quarters, yet determined not to retreat.

During this time we could not know what was taking place on other parts of the line. We were feeling rather exultant when, on looking to the left, we saw thousands of the blue coats pouring over the hill not 200 hundred yards away. They were sweeping back our lines like chaff before the wind.

It is said that our officers now, seeing the day lost, ordered a retreat. If so, we did not get the order, and continued to maintain the unequal contest, under a galling fire from both front and flank, until the two lines had almost enveloped us. Colonel Weeden, of our regiment, ordered all who could to save themselves.

The enemy were closing upon us from front and flank and so near as to order us to surrender. A portion of the regiment stacked arms, but what proportion I am unable, after so long a time, to say. Some of us, however, determined to escape, if possible. A race of half a mile for life and liberty through open, level fields to a range of hills covered with timber was our only hope. We ran in an oblique direction to avoid both lines. Some were killed immediately after leaving the stone fence and many others struck down within the first hundred yards. After that I have no recollection of seeing another member of the regiment. The ground had been frozen, but recently thawed which rendered it very laborious running and many were so exhausted they had to surrender. I passed a ditch or gully where a hundred or more Confederates had taken refuge and, at my suggestion that they had better be "making tracks" replied that they could not run a step further and were compelled to give it up.

By the time we reached the hills, our squad was reduced to about half a dozen, the remainder who were not disabled or captured having taken some other route. Here the writer had a close call but no damage was done except to disfigure my new uniform which I had worn just one month.

We climbed about half way up the hill, which was very high and steep, to some large trees where we took cover long enough to recover breath and view the scene below. The Federals had broken into a disorganized mob and the fields were dotted with blue coats as far back as we could see. Having left the stone fence with empty guns, we loaded while resting and fired on the enemy, some of whom had reached the foot of the hill. We then retreated further up, loaded, and fired again which had a tendency to check their advance, repeating the same tactics until we were enabled to gain the top.

Seeing they had abandoned their pursuit, so far as we were concerned, we sat down on a log for a good long rest. From our elevated position we had a good view of all that was going on below. Lee's corps, which had been on our right, making a gallant retreat against tremendous odds, firing volleys, falling back and firing again. It was a grand spectacle, but distressing to us, as we sat there and thought of the dead and dying comrades in the valley below. We thought, too, of the crushing defeat we had suffered, and the train of consequences which must inevitably follow.

When Lee's corps had been driven out of our right, around the base of the hill, it was becoming dark and began to rain. We struck our through the woods but, owing to the intense darkness, could only guess the direction to take and felt like we were about as liable to run into the enemy as our own men. After wandering over hills and hollows, woods and fields till 10 o'clock, we came into the Franklin pike at Thompson Station. The road was full of struggling soldiers like ourselves, all bent on making the distance between them and Nashville as long as possible by daylight. With no officers to command, we continued the retreat all night—every fellow for himself. We arrived at Franklin in the morning where the commissaries were issuing rations lavishly, having no wagons to haul it away, but warned us to be frugal as we might never have another chance at a Confederate commissary. A portion of the consolidated regiment got together here, officers took command and the continuing retreat was more orderly.

The enemy did not press us as much as might have been expected, but we had a dreary march through mud and slush for the next day or two. The weather changed from rain to sleet and our clothes froze on us, with many of the boys being bare-footed or nearly so and in this condition we footed it to Pulaski where we arrived on December 21st. Stragglers continued to come in during the night and by the next morning all who were fortunate enough to make their escape from Nashville had assembled. Roll call developed the fact that the 27th Alabama was almost completely wiped out. Of the one thousand who had left home just three years before, only seventeen were present including the line officers. I counted them and entered the number in my diary, so feel sure it is correct. Of the seventeen, about one half were company officers, leaving not more than eight or nine privates and non-commissioned officers. I made no entry concerning the consolidated regiment, consequently I cannot say how many of the 35th and 49th Alabama were present.

Three years before we had enlisted as twelve-month volunteers, little thinking then that we were entering on such a long and bloody struggle. We had endured hardships and dangers which often times seemed more than we could bear, but there was a function in the life of a soldier which compensates in large measure for the suffering and inconveniences to which we were subjected. Although deprived of comfortable clothing, often destitute of sufficient food, unsheltered from winter winds and snows, we were usually cheerful and buoyed up by the hope of accomplishing the object for which we were battling. The memories of past misfortunes and the desperate condition of affairs at that time seemed to concentrate themselves in an overwhelming weight of woe. The future seemed almost hopeless. Our armies were constantly retreating before innumerable, fresh and fully equipped troops. Worn out with hardship and fatigue, hunger and cold, we were in poor condition to bear the vicissitudes of the winter, which was upon us. With no material from which to recruit and little provision for those who had survived the outlook was gloomy indeed.

If the roll of the one thousand had been called and answers could have been heard, many would have come from Northern soil, of those who had succumbed to disease contracted in Northern prisons; many more from fields flush with victory; from scenes dark with dire defeat; whose bodies were moldering upon the battlefields of Mississippi, Georgia and Tennessee. Still others would have answered from widely scattered graves in our own Southland, where the gray moss waved in sympathy and the soft winds whispered a ceaseless requiem through the moaning pines. Now, of those who had survived the hundred days battles and skirmishes of the Georgia campaign and the Slaughter of Franklin, all, except a mere handful had yielded to overwhelming numbers and were again on their way to Northern prisons.

The little remnant of the regiment was furloughed and started home in advance of the command. The army followed the same day and crossed the Tennessee River at Bainbridge, six miles above Florence, through the 25, 26 and 27th of December 1864. Believing that General Hood would rest, for a few days at least, on the south side of the river, those of us who were on furlough were contentedly enjoying the Christmas days with homefolk. This was the first Christmas we had spent at home for three years, but instead of halting, he continued his march into Mississippi, thence to the Carolinas. We had been at home just two days when General Wilson, with 20,000 Federal cavalry came down on us like an avalanche and to our consternation went into winter quarters from Florence to Waterloo with headquarters at Gravelly Springs. The river was closely guarded from Decatur, Alabama to Clifton, Tennessee, a distance of 100 miles, and thus we were effectually cut off inside the enemy's line.

Members of other regiments were in the same unfortunate position, and every attempt to cross the river resulted in complete failure and in some instances the capture of the party. We had a strenuous time dodging the raiding parties, which were daily scouring the hills, hollows and thickets, but we were fortunate enough to elude them. We kept a constant vigil, all the time hoping for a chance to escape across the river, but the opportunity did not occur until too late to reach our command which was then in South Carolina. Owing to these unavoidable environments, I am unable to give but a meager history of the regiment after December 26, 1864. General Joseph E. Johnston had superseded General Hood and with a small force was confronting General Sherman in the Carolinas. The army of Tennessee was transferred to that department as rapidly as the crippled condition of transportation would permit. The consolidated regiment was again consolidated with the 55th and 57th Alabama and took part in the battles and skirmishes in North Carolina, the last battle being fought at Bentonville, March 19, 1865, resulting in a victory for our little army.*

As is well known the last act in the drama was played and the curtains lowered on the 26th of April 1865, when our great commander, General J. E. Johnston, surrendered to General W. T. Sherman.

At the close, Colonel Jackson commanded the remnant of the brigade, Colonel McAlexander the regiment, and our faithful Chaplain, Reverend Claiborne Coffee, was there to invoke divine blessings upon the heroic little band of survivors.

* In Serial 98, page 1063, it will be seen that the 27th Alabama was consolidated with the 35th, 49th, 55th, and 57th Alabama, under Colonel Edward McAlexander, and was put in General Shelley's brigade of Loring's division. The consolidation took place on April 9, 1865. Also see pages 1089, ibid., and Serial 100, page 773. Ed.

Closing Comments

I am indebted to the Honorable Henry A. Killen (now a member of the Alabama Legislature—1906) for the only information I have been able to get as to members of the regiment who were present at the surrender. In a letter of June 1906, he says seven company officers and two privates were paroled as follows: Capt. Rogers and Lt. H. Robinson, of Franklin County; Lt. Stoval, of Morgan County; Lieutenants J. H. Chandler, H. A. Killen, Sterling Brown and Wils Vaden, all of Lauderdale County; and Privates George Bowen and J. Hambrick, both of whom were wounded at Bentonville. These are all that Lt. Killen can remember, probably there are others and, if so, I regret that their names cannot be procured.

The regiment served three years and four months in eight states: Kentucky, Tennessee, Alabama, Mississippi, Louisiana, Georgia and North and South Carolina; was engaged in more than twenty battles besides hundreds of skirmishes, some of which were almost as destructive to the small number engaged as many of the battles fought. There were but few members of the regiment who did not, at some time during the war, serve a term in prison, and a large majority of them were in prison at the close, having been captured at Nashville, Tennessee on December 15 and 16, 1864.

Battles of the 27th Alabama

No more befitting conclusion to this imperfect history of the 27th Alabama can be made than to record a list of engagements in which the regiment, or parts of it, participated (omitting the many skirmishes and picket fights, which would be tedious to mention).

Bombardment of Fort Henry,	Feb. 6, 1862
Battles of Fort Donelson,	Feb. 12–16, 1862
Battle of Perryville, Ky.	Oct. 8, 1862
Bombardment of Port Hudson, La.	Jan.–April 1863
Battle of Baker's Creek, Miss.	May 16, 1863
Battles of Jackson, Miss.	July 8–17, 1863
Capture of the White Horse Co.	April 13, 1864
Battle of Resaca, Ga.	May 13, 1864
Battle of Cassville, Ga.	May 18, 1864
Battle of New Hope Church	May 25, 1864
Battle of New Hope Church	May 29, 1864
Battle of Kennesaw Mountain	June 15, 1864
Battle of Kennesaw Mountain	June 18, 1864
Battle of Kennesaw Mountain	June 24, 1864
Battle of Kennesaw Mountain	June 27, 1864
Battle of Peach Tree Creek	July 20, 1864
Battle of Atlanta, Ga.	July 28, 1864
(Poor-House or Lick Skillet Road)	
Battle of Franklin, Tenn.	Nov. 30, 1864
Battle of Nashville, Tenn.	Dec. 15, 1864
Battle of Nashville, Tenn.	Dec. 16, 1864

Battle of Kinston, N.C.   March 1865
Battle of Bentonville, N.C.   March 19–21, 1865

Colonel James Jackson

Colonel James Jackson of the 27th Alabama regiment was a wealthy and prominent citizen of Lauderdale County, who represented it in the legislature at different times. He was an influential member of the House at the time of his enlistment which was as a private in the 4th Alabama. It is remarkable how he and, as so many other men in the Confederate army, endured the privations, hardships, scarcity and roughness of a Confederate soldier's fare, after having been accustomed to the comforts, bounty, and luxuries of a wealthy Southern home, during the war period.

On the 18th of June, 1864, on the Kennesaw line, a portion of his skirmishers were subjected to a galling destructive fire from some of the enemy sheltered in a nearby house. Upon being informed, Colonel Jackson took a band of men from his regiment and, gallantly leading them, drove the enemy from the house, thus relieving his skirmishers and saving their lives. But it was a costly affair for him, as the enemy so shattered his arm as to require its amputation. He had been wounded as a private of the 4th Alabama at Manassas.

His son, J. Kirkman Jackson is (1912) a prominent business man at Montgomery, after having been the popular Private Secretary of the governor's through several gubernatorial administrations; and who had also been Secretary of State for Alabama.

Appendix I

Roster of the 27th Alabama

ABERNATHY, JOHN	Pvt.	E
ACOCK, STEPHEN	Pvt.	A, E
ADAMS, ANDREW J.	Pvt.	K, E
ADAMS, HENRY J.	Pvt.	C, E
ADAIR, ALBERT	Pvt.	D, E
ADAMS, JAMES P.	Pvt.	G
ADAMS, JOHN S.	Pvt.	-
ADAMS, T. T.	Pvt.	F, E
AGEE, W. A.	Cpl.	K, E
AIRY, J. A.	Pvt.	H, E
ALDRIDGE, NATHANIEL	Sgt.	D, E
ALEXANDER, E. M	1st Lt.	C
ALEXANDER, THOMAS	Pvt.	E
ALLEN, D. M.	Pvt.	D, E
ALLEN, H. D.	Sgt.	E, E
ALLISON, J. M.	Pvt.	B, E
AMOS, GEORGE W.	Pvt.	G, E
ANDERSON, J. R.	Pvt.	C, E
ANDERSON, NELSON	Pvt.	G, E
ANDERSON, SIDNEY S.	Capt.; Lt. Col.; Col.	G, E
ANDREW, ROBERT	1st Lt.; Capt.	E, E
ANDREWS, T. M.	Pvt.	E
ANGLE, WILLIAM N.	Cpl., Pvt.	B
ARMSTRONG, JAMES S.	Cpl.	F
ARMSTRONG, J. F.	Pvt.	C
ARNOLD, REASON B.	Pvt.	H, E
ASKEW, HENRY	Pvt.	A, E
ASKEW, JOHN	Pvt.	A, E
ASKEW, JOSEPH	Pvt.	A, E
ASTON, CHARLES J.	Pvt.	K, E
ATKINS, R. H.	Pvt.	I
AUSTIN, PHILLIP		
BACHAM, N.	Pvt.	H
BADGET, JAMES	Pvt.	G, E
BAKER, ANDREW T.	1st Sgt.; 4th Sgt.	B
BAKER, JOEL F.	Cpl., Pvt.	B
BALCOMBE, ALLEN	Pvt.	C
BALDING, J. T.	Sgt.	B, E
BALES, JOHN S.	1st Sgt.	F, E
BALLINGER, THOMAS M.	Pvt.	H, E
BARBER, J. M.	Cpl.	C, E
BARDEN, WILLIAM	Pvt.	A, E
BARKER, PETER	1st Lt.	A
BARKS, W. R.	Cpl.	D, E
BARNES, CLARK	Pvt.	F, E
BARNES, JAMES N.	Pvt.	K, E
BARNETT, J. A.	Asst. Surgeon	F & S
BARNETT, JAMES A.	Pvt.	I, E
BARNETT, J. W.	Pvt.	E, E
BARNETT, ZACHARIAH	Pvt.	E, E
BARNS, SHERD	Pvt.	H, E
BARON, HENLEY	Pvt.	H, E
BARUM, JOHN S.	Pvt.	D
BASS, EPHRUM	Pvt.	I, E
BASS, WILLIS	Pvt.	I, E
BATES, H. E.	Pvt., Cpl.	B, E
BAULKENER, ALLEN	Pvt.	C
BAYLES, JAMES M.	Pvt.	C & G, E

BAYLES, JAMES M. E.	Pvt.	C
BAYLES, JOHN H.	Pvt.	C, E
BAYLES, WILLIAM	Pvt.	G, E
BEAN, JAMES S.	Pvt.	G
BEARD, JAMES A.	Pvt.	F
BEAVER, A. J.	Pvt.	B, E
BEAVER, R. A.	Pvt.	K, E
BEAVER, W. C.	Sgt.	K, E
BECKWITH, A. W.	2 Lt.	C
BEDFORD, JESSE D.	Sgt.	C
BEDINGFIELD, J. D.	Pvt.	I, E
BEIONS, PATRICK	Pvt.	A
BELL, JESSE	Pvt.	F
BELLOIN, A. J.	Pvt.	G
BELSON, W. B.	Capt.	E, E
BENHAM, W. A.	Pvt.	I
BENTLEY, JOHN G.	2 Lt.	B
BETINGFIELD, JAMES	Pvt.	I
BEVIL, W. P.	Pvt.	F, E
BEVIS, A. J.	Pvt.	C, E
BEVIS, JESSE M.	Pvt.	-
BEVIS, T. F.	Pvt.	C, E
BIRD, B. S.	Pvt.	G
BLOCKSTOCK, WILLIAM C.	Pvt.	A, E
BLAIR, WILLIAM S.	Pvt.	I, E
BLEDSO, GEORGE W.	Cpl.	H, E
BORDEN, JAMES	Pvt.	K, E
BOUTLY, J. G.	(Bvt)2 Lt.	B
BOWDEN, TIMOTHY L.	Pvt.	A, E
BOWEN, E. B.	Pvt.	E, E
BOWEN, GEORGE O.	Cpl., Sgt.	G, E
BOWEN, J.	Pvt.	D
BOYCE, W. A.	1st Lt.	K, E
BOYD, J. B.	Pvt.	B
BOYD, JEFFERSON F.	Pvt.	B
BRACKEN, JOHN	Pvt.	K
BRADEN, H. A.	Pvt.	A
BRADFORD, JESSE D.	Sgt.	C, E
BRADLEY, J. C.	Pvt.	K, E
BRADLEY, JOHN	Pvt.	I
BRAGG, JAMES T.	Pvt.	F
BRAGG, L. H.	Pvt.	F, E
BRAGG, SANFORD C.	Pvt.	F
BRANCH, JOHN W.	Pvt.	F, E
BREWER, S.	(NCS) Drum Major	E
BRIDGES, JAMES	Pvt.	A, E
BRIDGES, JAMES A.	Pvt.	H, E
BRITNELL, J. W.	(Bvt.) 2 Lt.	A
BRITTON, G. H.	Pvt.	F, E
BRITTON, J. M.	Cpl.	F, E
BROCK, WILLIAM D.	Pvt.	G, E
BROGDEN, CLAIBORNE	Pvt.	H
BROOK, D. M.	Cpl.	K, E
BROOK, J. W.	Pvt.	K
BROOKS, C. C.	-	D
BROWN, ALBERT G.	Cpl., Pvt.	B
BROWN, FANTE P.	Pvt.	B
BROWN, GEORGE W.	Pvt.	A, E
BROWN, JAMES	-	-
BROWN, JANCEL	Pvt.	E
BROWN, JOHN L.	Pvt.	-
BROWN, J. W.	Cpl., Pvt.	D, E
BROWN, JOSEPH G.	Pvt.	G, E
BROWN, S. C.	1 and 2 Lt.	I, E
BROWN, W. H.	Pvt., 2 Lt.	D, C
BROWN, SAMUEL	Pvt.	D, E
BRUM, J. W.	-	-
BRYANT, EDWARD	Pvt.	C, E
BRYANT, WILLIAM	Pvt.	I
BRYANT, WILLIAM R.	Pvt.	H
BRYBER, MICHAEL A.	Pvt.	F, E
BULISON, EDWARD	Pvt.	F
BULLARD, NEWTON L. C.	Pvt.	G, E
BUNDY, WILLIS	Pvt.	I, E
BURDEN, ANDREW	Pvt.	D
BURDINE, R. B.	Pvt.	F, E
BURGE, WILLIAM	Pvt.	C, E
BURK, B. Y.	Pvt.	E, E
BURKE, SAMUEL D.	Pvt.	A, E
BURKS, WILLIAM	Pvt.	D
BURLESON, J. F.	Pvt.	B, E
BURLESON, W. M.	Pvt.	B, E
BURR, JAMES	Pvt.	C, E
BURROUGH, J. H.	Pvt.	E, E
BURRUS, T. P.	Pvt.	A, E
BUSH, SILAS	Pvt.	G, E
BUTCHER, J. W.	Cpl.	D, E
BUTLER, GABRIEL, JR.	Pvt.	I, E
BUTLER, GABRIEL, SR.	Pvt.	I, E
BUTLER, JOHN	Pvt.	A, E
BUTLER, J. W.	Pvt.	I
BUTLER, MINER V.	Pvt.	I
BYNUM, S. E.	Cpl.	E, E
BYRD, AKREL T.	Pvt.	F, E
BYRD, ISAAC W.	Pvt.	F, E
BYRNE, J.	Pvt.	F
CAGLE, J.	Pvt.	E, E
CALLAHAN, H. C.	Pvt.	I, E
CALLYHAN, HENRY	Pvt.	D, E
CALVERT, J.	Pvt.	H
CAMEL, B. W.	Pvt.	F
CAMPBELL, A.	Pvt.	F, E
CAMPBELL, M.	Pvt.	F, E
CAMPBELL, S.	Pvt.	F, E
CAMPBELL, WILLIAM T.	Pvt.	H, E
CAMPER, B. F.	Pvt.	D, E
CANADA, STARLING	Pvt.	C, E
CANADA, W. A.	Cpl.	C, E
CANNON, CALOP B.	Pvt.	B
CANNON, E. N.	Pvt.	C, E

CANNON, JAMES M.	Pvt.	B
CANNON, J. P.	Pvt.	C, E
CANNON, W. A.	Sgt.	B
CANNON, WILLIAM A.	Cpl.	B
CARGILL, A. C.	Fife Major	F&S, E
CARLISLE, FRANCIS J.	Pvt.	I, E
CARMICHAEL, DAVID	Pvt.	F, E
CARMICHAEL, GEORGE	Pvt.	F
CARR, JACKSON J.	Pvt.	E
CARR, JAMES J.	Pvt.	I, E
CARR, JOSEPH M.	Pvt.	G, E
CARR, MILTON	Pvt.	C
CARTER, ELIAS G.	Pvt.	H, E
CARTER, J. C.	Pvt.	B
CARTER, JOHN W.	Pvt.	G
CARTER, REUBEN R.	Pvt.	F, E
CARTER, W. J.	Pvt.	F
CASEY, SAMUEL GIPSON	Pvt.	C
CASSADY, SAMUEL	Pvt.	D
	(ALSO 27TN. INF.)	
CHAFFAN, J.	Pvt.	B
CHANDLER, JAMES H.	1 Lt.	C
CHANDLER, M. T.	Pvt.	I, E
CHANDLER, W. J.	Pvt.	I, E
CHANELL, JAMES T.	Pvt.	G, E
CHANNELL, HENRY J.	Pvt.	G, E
CHAPMAN, J. H.	Pvt.	K, E
CHILDRES, J. G.	Pvt.	K, E
CHINAULT, JAMES	Pvt.	D, E
CHISHOLM, DANIEL	Pvt.	B
CHURM, DAVID W.	Pvt.	H
CLANTON, JESSE	Pvt.	C, E
CLANTON, JOSEPH	Pvt.	C
CLARK, ELI	Pvt.	H
CLARK, JOHN S.	Pvt.	F, E
CLARK, SAMUEL	Cpl.	C, E
CLARKE, THOMAS	Pvt.	A, E
CLAUGH, GEORGE W.	Pvt.	A, E
CLAUNCH, D. J.	Pvt.	G, E
CLINTON, ISAAC	Pvt.	C
COAN, JAMES E.	Pvt.	G, E
COCHRAN, COLLINS W.	Pvt.	A, E
COCKBURN, WILLIAM	Sgt.	G,F&S,E
COFFEE, C. M.	Chaplain	F & S
COFFEE, N. T.	Pvt., Sgt. I, F&S, E	
COLEMAN, ALBERT	Pvt.	I, E
COLSTON, WILLIAM W.	Pvt.	C
COMER, J. W.	2 Lt.	I
COMMANDER, JESSE S. F.	Pvt.	I, E
CONDREY, DENIS	Pvt.	G, E
CONLEY, JOHN	Pvt.	H
CONLEY, U.	Pvt.	H
CONNAWAY, HIRAM T.	Pvt.	H, E
CONNELLY, JOHN W.	Pvt.	F
CONNER, A. J.	Sgt.	E, E
COOK, JAMES	Pvt.	G
COOK, J. D.	Pvt.	F, E
COOK, J. J.	Pvt.	F
COOK, S. V.	Pvt., Cpl.	C, E
COOK, W. C.	Pvt.	F, E
COOK, WILLIAM	Pvt.	G, E
COOPER, A. H.	Pvt.	D, E
COOPER, J. P.	Cpl.	D, E
COOPER, J. T.	Cpl.	D, E
COOPER, THOMAS M.	Sgt.	G, E
COOPER, WILLIAM	Pvt.	D, E
CORN, JOHN B.	Bvt., 2 Lt., Capt.	F
CORUM, THORNTON	Pvt.	I
COTHRON, W. MONROE	Pvt.	C, E
COTTON, JOHN	-	C
COTTRELL, G. W.	Cpl.	E
COWLES, URIAH,	-	H
COX, C. H.	Pvt.	B, E
COX, HIRAM	Cpl.	E
COX, JAMES A.	Pvt.	B
COX, J. M.	Cpl., Surgeon	B, E
COX, W. E.	Pvt.	H
COX, WILLIAM	Pvt.	B
COXWILL, JAMES R.	Pvt.	H, E
CROFT, ABSOLEM	Pvt.	K, E
CRAGS, MCGARDY	Pvt.	K, E
CROWFORD, ELBERT	Pvt.	K, E
CROWFORD, J. T.	Pvt.	A
CREAMER, JASPER	Pvt.	G, E
CREAMER, WILLIAM	Pvt.	G
CRINER, W. C.	2nd Lt.	F
CROCKER, WILLIAM W.	Pvt.	F, E
CROFT, W. C.	Lt.	I
CRONEY, BENJAMIN	Pvt.	I
CRONEY, NOAH	Pvt.	I, E
CRONEY, W. P.	Pvt.	I, E
CROOKS, SAMUEL B.	Pvt.	C
CROSS, J. A.	Pvt.	E, E
CROSS, J. B.	Pvt.	B
CROWSON, JOHN	Pvt.	I, E
CROWSON, W. P.	Cpl.	I
CRUCEL, JOHN T.	Pvt.	B
CRUCEL, JOSHUA D.	Pvt.	B
CRUMP, W. G.	Cpl.	E, E
CRUTCHER, JOHN B.	1 Lt.	F, E
CRUTCHER, W. H.	Pvt.	F, E
CRYSER, PATE	Pvt.	H
CUBSTEAD, HENRY C.	Pvt.	I, E
CULPEPER, THOMAS J.	Pvt.	H, E
CULPEPPER, JOEL M.	Sgt.	B
CUNNINGHAM, G. W	2 Lt.	E, E
CUNNINGHAM, J. M.	1 Sgt.	I, E
CUNNINGHAM, J. W.	1 Sgt.	I, E

CURETON, JAMES W.	Sgt.	H, E	EADY, CHARLES	-	-
DADON, M. W.	Lt.	I, H	EAST, WILLIAM	2 Lt.	G
DALRYMPLE, T. W.	Pvt.	C, E	EATON, S. K.	Sgt.	A, E
DANFORD, JOHN M.	Pvt.	G, E	EDWARDS, G. B.	Pvt.	E
DANIELS, C.	Pvt.	B	EGLESTON, G. B.	Pvt.	A, E
DANIELS, D. C.	Lt. Col.	F & S	ELLIS, CHARLES C.	Pvt.	I, E
DARRILL, JOHN	Pvt.	F	ELLIS, EDWIN T.	Pvt.	E
DAUGHERTY, W. H.	1 Lt.	D	EMERSON, H. H.	Capt.	B
DAUGHTRY, HENRY C.	Pvt.	F, E	EMY, JOHN A.	Pvt.	B
DAVENPORT, GEORGE W.	Cpl.	B	ENGLE, E. H.	Sgt.	E, E
DAVENPORT, JOHN	Pvt.	K	ENGLISH, JAMES P.	Pvt.	E
DAVIDSON, JOSEPH D.	Pvt.	K	ETHEREDGE, JOSEPH F.	Pvt.	H, E
DAVIDSON, J. T.	Surgeon	F & S	ETHERIDGE, B. J.	Pvt.	D
DAVIDSON, R. A.	Sgt.	I, E	EZELL, D. CROCKETT	Pvt.	C, E
DAVIDSON, S. M.	Pvt.	I, E	FARLEY, STEPHEN	-	D
DAVIS, BARNEY J.	Pvt.	A, E	FARLEY, THOMAS W.	-	D
DAVIS, H. C.	Pvt.	B	FARRIS, B. M.	1 Lt.	D, E
DAVIS, HENRY S.	Pvt.	A, E	FAY, PATRICK	Pvt.	A, E
DAVIS, JOHN	-	H	FERGUSON, JAMES	Pvt.	I
DAWSON, J. G.	Pvt.	K, E	FIKE, JAMES A.	Sgt.	G, E
DAWSON, JOSEPH	Pvt.	K, E	FIKE, JOHN J.	-	G
DAWSON, ROBERT	Pvt.	K, E	FISHER, JACKSON	Pvt.	D, E
DEAN, JOSEPH C.	Pvt.	F, E	FLEMINGS, CHARLES	1 Sgt.	G
DEES, EDMOND	Pvt.	K, E	FLETCHER, J. W.	1 Sgt.	C, E
DEMPSY, JOHN T.	Pvt.	C, E	FLINT, GEORGE	Pvt.	C
DENNIS, JOHN W.	Pvt.	H, E	FLYNT, HENRY A.	Pvt.	C, E
DENNIS, W. A.	Lt.	C	FLYNT, JOHN	Cpl., Sgt.	C, E
DENSON, W. O.	Bvt., 2 Lt.	H	FORD, THOMAS C.	Pvt.	H
DERMENT, J. J.	Surgeon	F & S	FOREMAN, J. W.	Pvt.	B, E
DERRICK, ANDREW	Pvt.	G	FORESYTH, G. W.	Pvt.	E, E
DERRICK, W. Y.	Pvt.	D, E	FOSTER, A. C.	Pvt.	E, E
DAVENPORT, JOHN	Pvt.	K, E	FOSTER, THOMAS J.	Col.	F & S
DEWBERRY, JABEZ	Pvt.	C, E	FOWLER, GOOLEY F.	Musician	H, E
DILLARD, ELIJAH	Pvt.	I, E	FOWLER, JOHN C.	Pvt.	F
DILLON, TIMOTHY	Pvt.	H, E	FOWLER, WILLIAM J.	Pvt.	I, E
DOCKINS, RUBIN	Pvt.	C, E	FOXWORTH, LEVI	Pvt.	F, E
DODSON, W. S.	Pvt.	D	FRANKS, J. W.	Pvt., Sgt.	D, E
DORMAN, ANDREW J.	Pvt.	F, E	FREEMAN, G. W.	Pvt.	F, E
DOSS, W. R.	Pvt.	D	FREEMAN, JAMES M.	Pvt.	F
DOTSON, F. J.	Pvt.	A, E	FREEMAN, R. J.	Pvt.	K, E
DOTSON, JOSEPH	Pvt.	A, E	FREEMAN, WILLIAM D.	Pvt.	F
DOUGLAS, G. M.	Pvt.	F	FRENCH, B. M.	Pvt., Sgt.	K, E
DOUGLASS, N. H.	Cpl.	E, E	FRENCH, GARRETT	Pvt.	E
DOWDY, WILLIAM C.	Pvt.	C, E	FRENCH, JAMES	Pvt.	E, E
DOWNS, J. M.	2 Lt.	B	FRY, ALISON W.	1 Lt.	A, E
DRAKE, EPHRAM H.	Sgt.	B	FUEKS, JOHN	Pvt.	C & E
DRAKE, JABUS	Pvt.	G, E	FUEKS, MARIDA	Pvt.	E, E
DRIVER, SPERE H.	Pvt.	H, E	FULLER, AMOS	Pvt.	F, E
DUCKIN, REUBEN	Pvt.	C	FULLER, JAMES	Pvt.	K
DUNCAN, JONATHAN	Pvt.	F, E	FULTON, B.	Pvt.	F, E
DUNN, HENRY	Pvt.	G	FUQUA, W. J.	Pvt.	F, E
DUNN, HENRY H.	Pvt.	H	GARMANY, WILLIAM H.	2nd Lt.	A, E
DUNN, R. W.	Pvt.	G	GARRETT, W. J.	Pvt.	C, E
DYKES, J. T.	Pvt.	B, E	GARRIS, GEORGE W.	Pvt.	G, E
			GARVIN, L. A.	Pvt.	A

GARVIN, WILLIAM M.	Pvt.	C, E	HALL, ANDREW	Pvt.		F
GEHU, S. M.	Pvt.	E, E	HALL, J. G. H.	Steward	F & S, E
GENTRY, JAMES P.	Pvt.	B	HALL, W. H.	Pvt.	K, E
GENTRY, JOHN W.	Lt.	C	HALLUM, J. N.	Cpl.	A, E
GEORGE, JOHN S.	3 Sgt.	B	HAMBRICK, J. C.	Sgt.	F, E
GERRARD, WILLIAM G.	Pvt.	E	HAMBRICK, J. H.	Pvt.	F, E
GHORMLEY, J. W.	Pvt.	F, E	HAMBY, JAMES W.	Pvt.	A, E
GIBSON, A. G.	Sgt.	F, E	HAMIL, JOHN M.	2 Lt.	F
GIBSON, W. F. C.	Pvt.	B, E	HAMILTON, H. G.	Pvt.	G
GIBSON, W. T.	Pvt.	K	HAMPTON, JOHN T.	Pvt.	B
GILBERT, ALBERT G.	Pvt.	C	HAMPTON, ROBERT G.	1 Lt.	B
GILBERT, RICHARD	Pvt.	C, E	HANIE, MARION G.	Pvt.	A, E
GILBERT, W. B.	Pvt.	H	HARAWAY, BENJAMIN	Pvt.	I, E
GILL, W. B.	Pvt.	B, E	HARDY, CHARLES	Pvt.	-
GILLAND, HOYT	Pvt.	A	HARGET, JAMES	Pvt.	G, E
GILMORE, STARLING	Musician	F, E	HARGET, JOHN	Pvt.	G, E
GODFREY, J. H.	Pvt.	F	HARKENSMITH, ELIAS J.	Pvt.	A, E
GODWIN, ELDRIDGE D.	1st Sgt.	I, E	HARPER, G. A.	Pvt.	A
GOLD, J. N.	Pvt.	F	HARPER, JOHN W.	2 Lt.	H, E
GOLDEN, GEORGE W.	Pvt.	F	HARREL, THEODORE F.	2 Lt.	B
GOLDEN, J. K.	Pvt.	F, E	HARRIS, ASHER K.	Pvt.	-
GOOCH, R. H.	Pvt.	H, E	HARRIS, JOHN	Pvt.	-
GOODMAN, WILLIAM J.	Cpl.	H, E	HARRIS, R. N.	1 Lt.	F & G
GOODNER, B. C.	Pvt.	F, E	HARRISON, J. M.	Pvt.	E
GOODSON, NACE H.	Cpl.	G, E	HARROLL, JOHN F.	Pvt.	F, E
GOODWIN, F. LE B.	Capt.	A, E	HARTSELL, SOLOMON W.	Pvt.	H
GOTCHER, W. J.	Cpl.	A, E	HARVY, J. L.	Pvt.	D
GOUGH, THOMAS W.	Pvt.	A, E	HAWKINS, D. W.	Pvt.	F, E
GRAHAM, W.	Pvt.	B	HAWKINS, PHILIP	Pvt.	K, E
GRAHAM, WILLIAM B.	Pvt.	B	HAYNES, HENRY T.	2 Lt.	G
GRAMMAR, J. R.	Cpl.	C, E	HEINE, HENRY	Pvt.	A, E
GRAVES, A. S.	Asst. Surgeon	F & S	HELMS, JOEL	Pvt.	K
GRAY, JOHN	Pvt.	D, E	HELUISTON, PETER	Pvt.	B
GRAY, JOHN S.	Pvt.	A, E	HENDERSON, A. W.	Pvt.	H, E
GRAY, WILLIAM B.	Sgt.	D, E	HENDERSON, ISAAC T.	Pvt.	A, E
GREEN, ED.	Pvt.	E	HENDRIX, WHITFIELD B.	1 Sgt.	K, E
GREEN, J. C.	Pvt.	A	HENLEY, GEORGE	2 Lt.	A
GREEN, J. G.	Pvt.	A	HENLEY, JOHN D.	Pvt.	A, E
GREEN, LEONARD	Pvt.	E	HENLEY, THOMAS W.	Pvt., 2 Lt.	A
GREEN, W. T.	Pvt.	A, E	HENLY, P. H.	Lt.	A
GRIDER, J.	Pvt.	A	HENSON, JOHN	Pvt.	I
GRIFFIN, JOSEPH	Pvt.	H	HERNBY, WINSOR	Pvt.	H, E
GRIFFITH, B. D.	Pvt.	F, E	HERNDON, GEORGE W.	Pvt.	F, E
GRIFFITH, ELMORE W.	Pvt.	K, E	HERNDON, HIRAM	Pvt.	F, E
GRIMES, A. J.	Pvt.	K	HERRON, JOHN J.	Pvt.	I
GRIMES, GEORGE B.	Pvt.	C, E	HERSTON, SAMUEL	Pvt.	I, E
GRIMES, NICHOLAS M.	Pvt.	D, E	HICKMAN, JAMES H.	Pvt.	H
GRIMES, WILLIAM F.	Pvt.	K, E	HIGHFIELD, A. J.	Pvt.	K
GRIMMITT, T. B.	Pvt.	F	HIGHTOWER, JAMES E.	Cpl.	F, E
GRISHAM, B. A.	Sgt.	I, E	HILL, BRADFORD	Pvt.	F
GRISHAM, W. P.	Pvt.	I, E	HILL, WILLIAM	Pvt.	E
GRUSHAM, WILY	Pvt.	K	HILL, J. C.	Pvt.	F
HACKETT, THOMAS	Pvt.	C, E	HILLS, EDGAR	Pvt.	-
HALBERT, A. J.	Pvt.	I, E	HINDMAN, A. J.	Pvt.	D, E
HALDEN, RICHARD	Pvt.	G	HINDMAN, JESSE M.	Pvt.	A, E

HOLDEN, C. C.	Pvt.	E, E
HOLLAND, H. E.	Pvt.	B, E
HOLLAND, JAMES M.	Pvt.	B, E
HOLLAND, J. I.	Pvt.	B, E
HOLLAND, J. T.	Pvt.	B, E
HOLLAND, R.	2 Lt.	D
HOLLAND, WILLIAM W.	Pvt.	G, E
HOLLINGSWORTH, JOHN K.	Pvt.	G, E
HOLMES, BENJAMIN F.	Pvt.	G, E
HOLMES, HENRY	Pvt.	I, E
HOLT, J. T.	Pvt.	E
HOOD, W. C.	1 Sgt.	E
HOOKER, G. W.	Sgt.	A, E
HORN, DANIEL H.	Pvt.	I
HORRES, JAMES	Pvt.	-
HORTON, J. C.	Pvt., 3 Lt.	K
HORTON, J. M.	Pvt.	K, E
HOUSE, JAMES	Pvt.	E
HOUSTON, JOHN A.	Surgeon	-
HOWELL, T. F.	2 Lt.	B
HUDSON, JOHN D.	Pvt.	A
HUGHES, A. A.	Col.	F&S
HUGHES, W. R.	Sgt., Major	F&S, E
HUMPHREY, R. M.	Capt.	H
HUMPHRIS, S.	Pvt.	B, E
HUNT, J. H.	Pvt.	B, E
HUNT, WILLIAM A.	Pvt.	B, E
HUNT, WILLIS G.	Pvt.	G, E
HURLEY, G. W.	2 Lt.	A
HURLEY, POLK	Pvt.	A, E
HURN, JOHN	Pvt.	I, E
HURST, ROBERT	Pvt., 2 Sgt., 1 Sgt.	G, E
HURST, THOMAS A.	Pvt.	G
HURST, WILLIAM	Pvt., 4 Sgt.	G, E
HUTTO, GEORGE W.	Pvt.	H, E
HUTTO, JAMES W.	Pvt.	F, E
IRBY, P. M.	Pvt.	D, E
IRBY, T. M.	Pvt.	F
IRELAND, R.	Pvt.	D
IRWIN, H. B.	Capt.	D, E
ISHEL, HENRY	Pvt.	G
ISHELL, WM. A.	Bvt., 2 Lt., Capt.	G, E
JACKS, JOHN H.	Bvt., 2 Lt.	F, E
JACKSON, JAMES	Lt.Col., Col.	F&S, D
JAMES, CHARLES	Pvt.	E
JAMES, C. S.	Pvt.	B, E
JAMES, ISAAC S.	Pvt., Musician	D
JERKINS, RICHARD S.	Pvt.	H, E
JOHNSON, ANDREW P.	Pvt.	G.E
JOHNSON, D. T.	Pvt.	C
JOHNSON, EDWIN	Pvt.	E
JOHNSON, JAMES L.	Pvt.	H, E
JOHNSON, JARID, R.	Pvt.	H, E
JOHNSON, S. D.	Pvt.	A, E

JOHNSON, THOMAS E.	Pvt.	H, E
JOINER, T. Z.	Pvt.	E, E
JONES, C.	Pvt.	E
JONES, CASPER H.	Pvt.	H, E
JONES, J. H.	Pvt.	H
JONES, JAMES H.	Pvt.	G, E
JONES, JOHN P.	-	-
JONES, JOHN W.	Pvt.	C, E
JONES, JOSEPH	Pvt.	H, E
JONES, JOSEPH	Pvt.	I, E
JONES, NATHAN A.	Pvt.	C
JONES, R. H.	Asst. Surgeon	F&S, E
JONES, RICHMOND L.	Pvt.	K, E
JONES, T. A.	Capt.	E
JUDKINS, J. C., JR.	Capt.	I
JULIAN, ANTHONY G.	Pvt.	G
KANEDAY, JOSEPH	Pvt.	G, E
KEELAN, THOMAS O.	Pvt.	G
KEEN, P. W.	Cpl.	H, E
KEENER, J. S.	Pvt.	E, E
KELLER, A. H.	Q.M., Capt.	F&S, E
KELLEY, EMANUEL	Pvt.	H, E
KELLEY, GEORGE	Pvt.	I, E
KENNADAY, E.	Pvt.	D, E
KERBO, GEORGE	Pvt.	I, E
KERBO, M. W.	Pvt.	I, E
KEY, HEZEKIAH E.	Pvt.	F, E
KEYS, JOHN B.	Pvt.	A, E
KIKER, L. P.	Pvt.	A
KILLEN, D. D	Cpl.	E, E
KILLEN, D. M.	Pvt.	E, E
KILLEN, H.A.	1 Lt.	E, E
KIMBRO, BENJAMIN F.	Cpl.	G, E
KIMBRO, GEORGE W.	Cpl.	G, E
KIMBRO, MORELON	Pvt.	G
KING, BREWCE	Pvt.	K
KING, JAMES M.	Pvt.	I
KING, J. F.	Pvt.	G, E
KING, J. L.	Pvt.	A, E
KING, JOHN W.	Pvt.	G, E
KING, M. V.	Pvt.	A, E
KIRK, WILLIAM L.	Pvt.	-
KISER, L. B.	Pvt.	A
KNIGHT, BENJAMIN	Pvt.	I, E
KNIGHT, CHARLES A.	Pvt.	G, E
KYLE, WILLIAM T.	Pvt.	H
LAMAN, SAMUEL	Pvt.	H
LAMB, J. R.	Cpl.	F, E
LAMBERT, JOEL	Pvt., Cpl.	I, E
LAMMONS, MURDOCK	Pvt.	F, E
LANDERS, FELIX	Pvt.	K, E
LANDERS, ISAAC C.	Pvt.	C
LANDERS, JACOB	Pvt.	A, E
LANDERS, JAMES	Pvt.	K, E
LANDERS, JAMES	Pvt.	A

LANDTROOP, JOHN	Pvt.	E, E	
LANE, REUBEN H.	Capt.	H, E	
LANGFORD, JOSEPH E.	Pvt.	C, E	
LANGFORD, W. DRAYTON	Pvt.	C, E	
LARENCE, WILLIAM L.	Pvt.	H	
LAUDERDALE, D. L.	Pvt.	E, E	
LAUGHINGHOUSE, J. W.	Pvt.	F	
LAWRENCE, THOMAS	Pvt.	H	
LAWSON, JOSEPH W.	Pvt.	G, E	
LEADBETTER, J. W. O.	Pvt.	B, E	
LEDBETTER, M. T.	Sgt.	C, E	
LEE, WILLIAM	Pvt.	F, E	
LEHR, WILLIAM	Pvt.	F, E	
LEONARD, WILLIAM	Pvt.	A	
LESLIE, MARTIN B.	Sgt.	A, E	
LILES, JAMES	Pvt.	E, E	
LILES, STEPHEN	Pvt.	E, E	
LINDSAY, AID	Pvt.	C, E	
LINDSAY, A. J.	Pvt.	C, E	
LINDSEY, R. M.	1 Sgt., 1 Lt.	B	
LINER, MARION	Pvt.	A, E	
LINSEY, MONROE	Pvt.	C	
LOGAN, WASHINGTON	Pvt.	G, E	
LONG, JOHN	Pvt.	C, E	
LONG, JOSEPH	Pvt.	G, E	
LOONY, JOHN	Pvt.	F	
LOTT, ARTHUR	Pvt.	G, E	
LOUIS, HANSON	Pvt.	G, E	
LOVE, THOMAS J.	Pvt.	C, E	
LOVELACE, ASA	Pvt.	C, E	
LOVELACE, HAZEL L.	Pvt.	C, E	
LOWREY, ADAM	Sgt.	A, E	
LUCKY, RICHARD	Pvt.	-	
LYLE, E. F.	Pvt.	H	
MABERRY, A. P.	1 Sgt.	D	
MACHEN, MARION H.	Pvt.	D	
MAGNESS, L. H.	Pvt.	A, H	
MALONE, A. J.	Pvt.	F, E	
MALONE, J. W.	Pvt.	F, E	
MALONEY, A. M.	-	D	
MALOY, V. P.	Pvt.	B, E	
MANDLEY, W. E.	2 Lt.	D, E	
MANING, J. D.	Pvt.	A	
MANN, THOMAS	Pvt.	F	
MARION, PEAK F.	Pvt.	H	
MARONEY, MIDDLETON	Pvt.	G, E	
MARTIN, A.	Pvt.	C, E	
MARTIN, FRANCIS M.	Pvt.	G, E	
MARTIN, W.	Pvt.	I	
MARTINDALE, JOSEPH F.	Cpl.	I	
MASSEY, R. H.	Pvt.	E	
MAXWELL, J. W.	Pvt.	E, E	
MAY, ALEXANDER	Pvt.	F	
MAY, S. W.	Pvt.	A, E	
MAYBERRY, E.	Pvt.	D	
MAYES, JAMES H.	1 Sgt.	A, E	
MCALEXANDER, ED	Lt. Col., Col.	F&S	
MCCALL, J.	Pvt.	E, E	
MCCAMPBELL, JAMES A.	Pvt.	C, E	
MCCARLEY, JAMES	3 Lt.	H, E	
MCCARLEY, W. S.	Sgt.	H, E	
MCCARTNEY, C. W.	Pvt.	F, E	
MCCARTNEY, JAMES	Pvt.	I, E	
MCCARTNEY, ROBERT	Pvt.	I, E	
MCCLOUD, DANIEL	Pvt.	F, E	
MCCLUNG, J. H.	Pvt.	H, E	
MCCLUSKEY, T. B.	Pvt.	A, E	
MCCOLOUGH, T. E.	Capt.	G	
MCCORLEY, JAMES	Pvt.	H	
MCCORMICK, G. E.	Pvt.	I	
MCCOY, A. H. C.	Pvt.	F, E	
MCCOY, ALEX H.	Sgt.	F	
MCCRACKEN, J. E.	Sgt.	E, E	
MCCURLEY, JAMES	Pvt., 2 Lt.	H	
MCDANIEL, ELIJAH	Pvt., Cpl.	D, E	
MCDANIEL, J. C.	Pvt.	G	
MCDERMIT, JOSEPH	Pvt.	A, E	
MCELGEN, J. W.	Pvt.	F, E	
MCELROY, WILLIAM	Pvt.	F	
MCGARDEN, JAMES	-	F	
MCGEHEE, THOMAS M.	1 Lt., Capt.	K	
MCGHEE, H.A.	Capt.	I	
MCGHEE, SILAS	2 Lt.	I	
MCGILOVARY, MALCOM	Pvt.	G, E	
MCGRIN, R. L.	-	F	
MCGUYER, W. J.	Cpl.	A, E	
MCINHER, J.A.	Pvt.	E	
MCINNIS, PETER	Pvt.	G, E	
MCINTOSH, ANGUS	Pvt.	G, E	
MCINTYRE, A. J.	Pvt.	C, E	
MCINTYRE, DUNCAN	Pvt.	H, E	
MCKARKLE, LOUIS	Pvt.	G, E	
MCKINON, ALEXANDER M.	Pvt.	G, E	
MCMAHEN, J.A.	2 Lt.	E, E	
MCMAHEN, R.A.	Sgt.	F	
MCPOOLS, W. F.	Pvt.	H	
MCRAE, ALEXANDER R.	Pvt.	G, E	
MCRAE, DANIEL C.	Pvt.	G, E	
MCWILLIAMS, J.A.	Pvt.	A, E	
MCWILLIAMS, J. W.	Pvt.	A, E	
MEADOWS, B. F.	Asst. Surgeon	F&S	
MELSON, JOHN	Pvt.	D, E	
MELTON, GEORGE W.	Pvt.	K	
MESSINGER, ASA M.	Bvt. 2 Lt.	G, E	
MILES, SAMUEL R.	Cpl.	F&D, E	
MILES, W. J.	Pvt.	F	
MILLER, LANSFORD A.	Pvt.	B	
MILLER, WILLIAM M.	Pvt.	B	
MILLER, W. J.	Pvt.	F	
MILLS, C. B.	Pvt.	B, E	

MILLS, JOSEPH E.	Pvt.	F, E	OLIVE, JAMES J.	2 Lt.	C, E
MILTON, G. W.	Pvt.	K	OLIVER, DANIEL	Pvt.	A, E
MILWEE, C. S.	Pvt.	A, E	OLIVER, HIRHAM	Pvt.	A, E
MISSELDINE, JOHN K.	Pvt.	K	O'NEAL, MILTON C.	Cpl.	I, E
MITCHEL, ANANIAS	Pvt.	K, E	OREAR, D.	Pvt.	-
MITCHELL, A. S.	1 Lt.	C, E	OWEN, JOHN H.	Pvt.	I, E
MITCHELL, THOMAS J.	1 Lt.	A, E	OWEN, R. G.	2nd Lt.	H
MIXON, W. C.	1 Lt.	I	OWEN, SAMUEL	Pvt.	I, E
MOLT, WILLIAM	Pvt.	C	OWENS, LEWIS A.	Pvt.	B
MOODY, JAMES W.	Pvt.	C, E	PAGE, GEORGE W.	Pvt.	F
MOORE, ALLEN J.	Pvt.	B	PAGE, R. N.	Pvt.	F
MOORE, C. C.	Pvt.	A, E	PALMER, JAMES W.	Pvt.	C, E
MOORE, HENRY	Pvt.	G, E	PALMER, SAMUEL	Pvt.	C, E
MOORE, JAMES A.	Pvt.	H	PALMER, WILLIAM C.	Pvt.	C, E
MOORE, JAMES W.	Cpl.	A, E	PARIS, ELIAS C.	Pvt.	C, E
MOORE, J. E.	Capt.	A	PARKER, BLUFORD	Pvt.	D
MOORE, R. L.	Pvt.	F, E	PARKER, JOHN F.	Pvt.	B
MOORE, WILLIAM B.	Pvt.	B	PARKER, R.	Pvt.	D
MORGAN, W. W.	Pvt.	A	PARKMAN, GEORGE W. L.	Sgt.	F, E
MORLAND, HAYWOOD H.	Pvt.	G, E	PARKS, BUTLER M.	Pvt.	F, E
MORRIS, B. H.	Pvt.	H	PARKS, RALPH B.	Musician	F, E
MORTON, E.	Pvt.	E, E	PARSON, WILLIAM A.	Pvt.	F
MOSELEY, W. B.	Pvt.	F, E	PARTON, HUBBARD	Pvt.	G
MULINAX, WILLIAM	Pvt.	A, E	PATRICK, JAMES	Pvt.	I
MURDOCK, J. A. D.	Sgt.	E, E	PATRICK, J. J.	Pvt.	K
MURPHREE, JAMES	Capt. & Q.M.	F&S	PATRICK, JOHN W.	Pvt.	K
MURPHREE, JOEL DYER	Q.M., Sgt.	E	PATRICK, MARTIN	Pvt.	K
MURPHY, JOHN	Pvt.	A, E	PATTERSON, B.	2 Lt.	-
MURPHY, LOUIS	Pvt.	A, E	PATTERSON, G. S.	Pvt.	K
NAPIER, JAMES M.	2 Lt.	I	PATTERSON, ISAAC W.	Cpl.	F, E
NETHERLAND, JOHN M.	Pvt.	A, E	PATTERSON, JOHN W.	Pvt.	B
NEWBERRY, ALBERT H.	Pvt.	I, E	PATTERSON, JOSEPH G.	Pvt.	F, E
NEWSOM, SOLOMON	Sgt.	K, E	PAYNE, R. E.	Pvt.	D
NICHOLS, B. F.	Pvt.	K, E	PEACOCK, ASHLEY P.	Cpl.	F, E
NICHOLS, WILLIAM	Pvt.	I	PEACOCK, JOSEPH H.	Cpl.	I, E
NICHOLS, W. J.	Pvt.	D, E	PEACOCK, MOULTON C.	Pvt.	H, E
NICKLER, R. C.	Pvt.	K	PEAK, FRANCIS M.	Pvt.	H, E
NIX, PLEASANT	Cpl.	G, E	PEAK, L. H.	Pvt.	H, E
NIXON, J. B.	Pvt.	E, E	PEAK, MARSHAL	Pvt.	H, E
NIXON, WILLIAM H.	Pvt.	C, E	PEAK, S. D.	Pvt.	H, E
NOLEN, JESSE T.	Sgt.	A	PEARSON, JAMES A.	1st Lt.	K
NOLEN, R. W.	Pvt.	A, E	PECK, HENRY C.	Pvt.	H
NORMAN, WILLIAM C.	Pvt.	C, E	PEPPERS, HENRY C.	Pvt.	K, E
NORRIS, C. H.	Pvt.	F	PERKINSON, LAFAYETTE	Pvt.	I, E
NORRIS, WILLIAM	Pvt.	G, E	PERKINSON, WILLIAM	Pvt.	I, E
NORTON, JOHN J.	Pvt.	I, E	PETTEY, NEWTON E.	Sgt., Pvt.	F
NUGENT, JAMES	Pvt.	I	PETTUS, W. W.	1st Lt.	E
NUGENT, SAMUEL	Pvt.	I, E	PHILLIPS, CHARLES W.	Pvt.	C
NUNLEY, THOMAS	Pvt.	I, E	PHILLIPS, FRANKLIN	Pvt.	A, E
NUNNELLEY, PETER	Capt.	A, E	PHILLIPS, JOHN W.	Pvt.	C, E
ODEN, BRITTEN B.	Pvt.	E	PHILLIPS, SANFORD J.	Pvt.	G, E
ODOM, J. H.	Cpl.	D, E	PICKELSIMMER, JASON	Pvt.	D
ODOM, WATSON W.	Pvt.	C, E	PIERCE, G. W.	Pvt.	F
OLD, H. B.	Pvt.	D, E	PIGG, WILLIAM C.	Pvt.	B

PONDER, W. J.	2d Lt.	D, E		RITTER, JOHN	Pvt.	F
POOL, G. C.	Pvt.	C, E		RITTER, L. T.	Pvt.	E, E
POOL, JAMES M.	Pvt.	C, E		RITTLER, JOHN H.	Pvt.	E
POOL, NATHANIAL	Pvt., Sgt.	C, E		ROBERSON, J. B.	Pvt.	E, E
POOL, W. M.	Pvt.	B, E		ROBERSON, JOE	Pvt.	B, E
PORTWOOD, JESSE	Pvt.	A, E		ROBERSON, L. G.	Pvt.	B, E
POSEY, J. M.	Cpl.	D, E		ROBERTS, JOHN L.	Pvt.	B
POWELL, G. W.	Pvt.	D, E		ROBERTS, J. R.	Pvt.	D
POWELL, LEVI K.	Sgt.	F, E		ROBERTS, M. P.	Capt.	F
POWELL, PETER	Cpl.	D		ROBERTS, R. S.	Pvt.	H
PRATER, N. F.	Pvt.	B, E		ROBERTSON, COLUMBUS F.	Cpl.	A, E
PRICE, COSWELL	Pvt.	C, E		ROBINS, AUGUSTUS	Pvt.	B
PRICE, JAMES A.	Pvt.	D, E		ROBINSON, J. H.	2 Lt.	G, E
PRICHARD, WILLIAM	Pvt.	A, E		ROBINSON, JOHN	Pvt.	G, E
PRUITT, JOHN C.	Pvt.	C, E		RODGERS, R. C.	Pvt.	F, E
QUILLEN, WILLIAM	Pvt.	E, E		RODGERS, W. J.	Pvt.	F, E
RACHELS, JOHN J.	Pvt.	E		ROE, WILLIAM P.	-	E
RAINES, W. D.	Pvt.	G		ROGERS, I. J.	2 Lt., Capt.	B
RANDLE, WILEY N.	Sgt.	C, E		ROGERS, J. L.	Cpl.	B, E
RANDOLPH, ABRAHAM	Pvt.	K, E		ROGERS, PHILIP R.	Pvt.	H, E
RANDOLPH, J. B.	Pvt.	K		ROMINES, PETER	Pvt.	I, E
RANDOLPH, J. M.	Pvt.	K, E		RORAX, J. W.	Pvt.	E, E
RANDOLPH, J. T.	Pvt.	K, E		ROSE, B. F.	Pvt.	E, E
RANDOLPH, SAMUEL G.	Pvt.	K, E		ROSWELL, A. B.	Pvt.	F, E
RATCLIFF, C.	1 Lt.	H		ROTON, ARCHIE	Pvt.	K
RATCLIFF, J.	-	I		ROUNTREE, JOHN I.	Pvt.	G, E
RAY, A. S.	Sgt.	I, E		ROWAN, BAILY D.	Pvt.	B
RAY, HIRAM	Cpl.	I		RUCKER, GEORGE	Cpl., Sgt.	K
RAY, H. L.	Capt.	I, E		RUCKER, WILLIAM	Pvt.	K, E
RAY, H. L.	Pvt.	I, E		RUDD, JAMES D.	Pvt.	I, E
RAY, REILLY	Pvt.	I		RUSSELL, F. M.	Pvt.	H, E
REA, A. M.	Sgt.	G, E		RUSSELL, JAMES	Pvt.	G
REA, ROBERT	Pvt.	G, E		RUTLEDGE, JOHN O.	Pvt.	H
REA, WILLIS C.	Pvt.	G, E		RUTLEDGE, R. F.	Pvt.	H
READER, L. T.	Pvt.	E		RYAN, HENRY	1 Lt.	H, E
REATON, JOHN	Pvt.	-		RYAN, ISAAC	Pvt.	H
REED, JAMES J.	Pvt.	A		RYAN, THOMAS C.	Pvt.	H, E
REESE, JOHN	Pvt.	K		SAMMONS, BENJAMIN	Pvt.	D
REID, JOHN	Pvt.	K		SAMPLE, J. A.	Pvt.	H
RETHERFORD, D. R.	Pvt.	H, E		SAMS, JOHN C.	Pvt.	H, E
RETHERFORD, WILLIAM H.	Pvt.	H, E		SANDERS, AMOS A.	Sgt.	I, E
REYNOLDS, E.	(Col. prisoner)	H		SANDERS, JOHN R.	Pvt.	H, E
RHODES, N. S.	Pvt.	C, E		SANDERSON, DOUGLAS	Pvt.	K, E
RICE, M.	Bvt., 2 Lt.	F		SANSBURG, JOHN N.	Sgt.	F, E
RICHARDSON, BRYANT W.	Pvt.	C, E		SAPP, JOHN A.	Pvt.	D
RICHARDSON, JAMES	Bvt. 2 Lt.	E		SAPP, ROBERT W.	Pvt.	D, E
RICHARDSON, JAMES W.	Pvt.	C, E		SAWYERS, ALEXANDER T.	Musician	H, E
RICHARDSON, JEFFERSON L.	Pvt.	C, E		SCARBROUGH, E.	Pvt.	F
RICHARDSON, J. M.	Pvt.	E, E		SCHULTZ, WILLIAM A.	Sgt.	G
RICHARDSON, WILSON E.	Pvt.	K, E		SCOGINS, W. G.	Pvt.	K
RICHERSON, J. T.	Pvt.	A, E		SCOGINS, W. J.	Pvt.	K
RICHERSON, T. S.	Sgt.	A, E		SEGO, GEORGE W.	Pvt.	C, E
RIDER, A. C.	-	K		SELF, J.	Pvt.	H, E
RIGNEY, F. J.	Pvt.	F, E		SELLERS, HARDY	Pvt.	B

SELLERS, JOHN A.	Pvt.	B		SPELCE, JOHN	Pvt.	F
SHANE, BAYLISS B.	Pvt.	I, E		SPENCE, W. M.	Sgt.	C, E
SHARP, IRA	Pvt.	C, E		SPOTSWOOD, IRBY E.	Sgt.	D, E
SHARP, OWEN	Pvt.	-		SPRUILL, G. T.	Pvt.	E
SHAW, HARRIS	Pvt.	F, E		STAFFORD, ROBERT	Pvt.	G, E
SHEETS, T. B.	3 Lt.	D, E		STALLINGS, ZACHARIAH	Pvt.	H, E
SHELTON, GEORGE A.	Pvt.	-		STANFORD, F. M.	Pvt.	I
SHELTON, T. B.	Pvt.	E, E		STANFORD, MASON	Pvt.	I
SHEPPARD, JEFFERSON	Pvt.	K, E		STANLEY, THOMAS	Pvt.	G
SHERLEY, JOHN W.	Cpl.	B		STANPHILL, V. C.	Sgt.	B, E
SHIELDS, JEFFERSON J.	Pvt.	K, E		STANPHILL, W. P.	Pvt.	B, E
SHOEMAKER, CHARLES R.	Pvt.	I		STAUGHTER, WILLIAMS	Pvt.	G, E
SHOEMAKER, RICHARD	Pvt.	I, E		STEEL, ALSAM	Pvt.	A
SHOEMAKER, WILLIAM P.	Pvt.	B		STEEL, W. C.	Pvt.	G
SIMES, W. H.	Pvt.	E		STEPHENS, JAMES D.	Pvt.	G, E
SIMMONS, JAMES	Musician	G, E		STEPHENSON, WILLIAM	Pvt.	H
SIMMONS, JAMES M.	1 Sgt.	C		STEVENS, TUBAL C.	Pvt.	C
SIMMONS, JOHN	Pvt.	K		STEWART, C. D.	Chief Musician	E, E
SIMMONS, L. C.	Pvt.	K, E		STEWART, J. W.	Pvt.	G, E
SIMMS, G. W.	Pvt.	E, E		STINWIDER, J. E.	Pvt.	I
SIMPSON, W.	2 Lt.	G		STOKES, WILLIAM	Pvt.	K, E
SIMS, S. T.	Pvt.	G		STONE, W. M.	Pvt.	F, E
SIMS, WILLIAM W.	Pvt.	H, E		STOUT, PATRICK	Pvt.	-
SMITH, ALFRED B.	Pvt.	H, E		STOVALL, W. F.	2 Lt.	H, E
SMITH, ENOCH	Pvt.	H		STRICKER, HENRY	Pvt.	L
SMITH, G. W.	Pvt.	A, E		STRICKLIN, LOTT	Pvt.	G, E
SMITH, ISAC D.	Pvt.	G, E		STRINGER, WILLIAM M.	Pvt.	H, E
SMITH, JAMES A.	Pvt.	B		STRONG, ROBERT N.	Sgt.	F, E
SMITH, JOHN H.	Pvt.	H		STUART, JOHN B.	Capt.	H, E
SMITH, JOHN P.	Pvt.	I & D		STUNGER, BENJAMIN B.	Pvt.	G
SMITH, JOSEPH	Pvt.	A, E		STUNGER, MATHEW B.	Cpl.	B
SMITH, JOHN R.	Pvt.	C, E		SUGG, JAMES	Pvt.	G, E
SMITH, LEROY	Pvt.	G		SUMMERHILL, WILLIAM R.	Cpl.	C, E
SMITH, LEVI	Pvt.	K, E		SURNER, A. J.	Pvt.	D
SMITH, SAMUEL J.	Pvt.	H, E		SUTHERLAND, WILLIAM N.	Pvt.	-
SMITH, SAMUEL W. W.	Pvt.	K, E		SWEATMAN, J. B.	Pvt.	G, E
SMITH, THOMAS	Pvt.	H		TATUM, J. H.	Pvt.	H
SMITH, WILLIAM T.	Pvt.	G, E		TAYLOR, JACKSON	Pvt.	A, E
SMITH, WILLIAM R.	1 Sgt.	G, E		TAYLOR, J.	-	A
SMITH, W. M.	2 Lt.	A		TAYLOR, LEMICK	Pvt.	G, E
SMITHEY, U.	Pvt.	F		TAYLOR, RICHARD	Pvt.	G, E
SMOTHERMAN, J. T.	Pvt.	H		TAYLOR, STEPHEN H.	Pvt.	B
SNEED, E. B.	Pvt.	F, E		TAYLOR, THOMAS J.	1 Sgt.	I
SNEED, J. R.	Pvt.	F, E		TAYLOR, T. J.	Pvt.	G
SNEED, W. W.	Pvt.	F, E		TAYLOR, W. H.	Pvt.	E, E
SNELL, ELLIS W.	Pvt.	F, E		TAYLOR, WILLIAM	Pvt.	B
SNELL, VANDY V.	Pvt.	F, E		TEAGUE, JAMES R.	Pvt.	A, E
SNELLGROVE, WILLIAM J.	Sgt.	I, E		TEAL, DANIEL	Pvt.	G, E
SNIDER, JAMES A.	Pvt.	H, E		TERRELL, RICHARD	Pvt.	C, E
SNODGROSS, THOMAS	Pvt.	I, E		TEW, HESEKIA	Cpl.	G, E
SOOT, BENJAMIN S.	1 Lt.	F		TEW, JAMES A.	Pvt.	G, E
SORRELL, JOHN	Pvt.	I, E		TEW, PETER F.	Pvt.	G, E
SOUTHERLIN, W. N.	Cpl.	K		THIGPEN, A. M.	Pvt.	E
SPANGLER, J. W.	1 Sgt.	K, E		THIGPEN, R. F. M.	Pvt.	E, E
SPEER, W. T.	Cpl.	A, E		THOMAS, N. A.	Pvt.	C

THOMAS, SOLOMON	Sgt.	K, E		WARREN, E. T.	1 Lt.	D
THOMAS, WILLIAM	Pvt.	I, E		WATKINS, JONATHAN D.	Pvt.	H
THOMPSON, E. B.	Capt.	C, E		WATKINS, J. W.	-	E
THOMPSON, JAMES	Pvt.	E, E		WATKINS, R. J.	Pvt.	D, E
THOMPSON, R. M.	Pvt.	B, E		WATSON, DAVID G.	Pvt.	B
THOMPSON, W. A.	1 Sgt.	C, E		WATSON, D. S.	Pvt.	K, E
THORN, WILLIAM H.	Pvt.	B		WATSON, JOHN T.	Pvt.	D, E
THORNTON, JOHN	Pvt.	I, E		WATSON, R. H.	1 Lt.	B, E
THORNTON, JOHN T.	Pvt.	F, E		WATSON, T. M.	Pvt.	G
THRASHER, J. H.	Cpl.	E, E		WATSON, W. S.	-	POW
THRASHER, M. J.	Pvt.	E, E		WATTS, JOHN W.	Pvt.	B
TIDWELL, SAMUEL	Pvt.	C, E		WEBB, J. N.	Pvt.	F, E
TILLIS, TEMPLE	Pvt.	K, E		WEBB, THOMAS J.	Pvt.	B
TOLIVER, J. E.	Pvt.	D, E		WEBB, WESLEY W.	Pvt.	B
TOMLIN, WILLIAM R.	Pvt.	H, E		WEBSTER, J. A.	Pvt.	B
TOWNSEND, B. F.	Pvt.	A, E		WEEKS, WILLIAM H.	Pvt.	H, E
TREADWAY, ELIAS	Pvt.	B		WEEMES, J. W.	Pvt.	K, E
TRIBBLE, JOHN	Pvt.	I, E		WELLS, R.	Pvt.	B
TRICE, JAMES T.	Sgt.	A, E		WERSON, RANDOLPH	Pvt.	C
TUCKER, GEORGE W.	Pvt.	B		WESLEY, WILLIAM	Pvt.	K, E
TUCKER, WILEY	Pvt.	B		WESSON, WILLIAM	Pvt.	C
TURNER, W. R.	Pvt.	A, E		RANDOLPH		
VADEN, F. M.	Pvt.	B, E		WEST, COLUMBUS C.	Pvt.	B
VADEN, M. W.	Cpl., Bvt. 2 Lt.	I, E		WESTBROOK, JOHN M.	Pvt.	G, E
VANDOVER, G. W.	Pvt.	K, E		WHEELER, A. L.	Capt.	C, E
VEACH, STEPHEN D.	Pvt.	B		WHISNANT, HENRY	Pvt.	G, E
VICK, CHARLES J.	Pvt.	B		WHITE, R. G.	Pvt.	F
WADE, JOHN H.	Pvt.	H, E		WHITE, W. C.	Pvt.	F, E
WADE, THOMAS	Pvt.	H, E		WHITEHURST, JESSE	Pvt.	H, E
WAGGNER, W. M.	Pvt.	K		WHITHEAD, JONES	Pvt.	I, E
WAITS, SHELTON A.	Pvt.	C, E		WHITLOCK, WILLIAM	Pvt.	A, E
WALDEN, JORDAN	Pvt.	G, E		WIDENER, MOSES P.	Pvt.	H
WALDEN, RICHARD	Pvt.	G, E		WILBANKS, JAMES A.	Pvt.	I, E
WALDIN, PATRICK	Pvt.	F, E		WILKES, WILLIAM H.	Pvt.	G, E
WALDING, BENJAMIN V.	1 Lt.	H, E		WILKINSON, O. T.	Pvt.	C, E
WALDROP, EDMOND	Pvt.	K, E		WILLIAMS, A. C.	Pvt.	H, E
WALDROP, JASPER	Pvt.	E, E		WILLIAM, CALEB	Pvt.	G, E
WALDROP, WATSON	Cpl.	K, E		WILLIAMS, JAMES G.	Pvt.	H, E
WALKER, J. E.	Pvt.	D		WILLIAMS, J. J.	Pvt.	E, E
WALKER, T. C.	Pvt.	E, E		WILLIAMS, J. T.	Pvt.	E
WALKER, WELBEM	Pvt.	G, E		WILLIAMS, JOHN W.	Pvt.	H, E
WALLACE, GEORGE H.	2 Lt.	K		WILLIAMS, LOUIS C.	Cpl.	I, E
WALLACE, J. P.	Pvt.	A		WILLIAMS, O. P.	Pvt.	E, E
WALLACE, J. W.	Pvt.	C, E		WILLIAMS, PRESLEY	Pvt.	I, E
WALLACE, SAMUEL	Pvt.	I, E		WILLIAMS, R. C.	1 Sgt.	H, E
WALLACE, S. M.	Pvt.	C, E		WILLIAMS, S. A.	-	I
WALLACE, W. A.	Pvt.	C, E		WILLIAMS, WILLIAM W.	Pvt.	B
WALLACE, W. H.	Pvt.	A		WILLIAMSON, A. H.	Pvt.	F
WALLACE, W. J.	Pvt.	C, E		WILLIAMSON, ANDREW S.	Pvt.	H, E
WALTON, T. H.	Pvt.	E		WILLIAMSON, HENRY	Pvt.	G, E
WAMACK, JAMES M.	Pvt.	F		WILLIAMSON, THOMAS	Pvt.	G
WARD, G. B.	Pvt.	B, E		WILLIAMSON, WILLIAM A.	Pvt.	H, E
WARD, TOLLIVER	Pvt.	H, E		WILLS, RANSOM	Pvt.	B
WARHURST, J. M.	Pvt.	A, E		WILLSON, P. W.	Cpl.	K
WARHURST, S. F.	Pvt.	A, E		WILSON, H. B.	Pvt.	D, E

WILSON, WILLIAM	Pvt.	G
WILSON, WILLIAM C.	Pvt.	I, E
WINBOURN, H. G.	Sgt.	C, E
WINDHAM, THOMAS	Pvt.	F, E
WINDHAM, WRIGHT P.	1 Sgt.	F, E
WINEDEN, JAMES L.	Pvt.	H
WINFREY, J. M.	Pvt.	D, E
WINGET, RICHARD E.	-	E
WINSTEAD, WILLIAM	Pvt.	G
WOOD, ANDERSON M.	Pvt.	D
WOOD, J. P.	Maj. Appointment	-
WOOD, T. J.	Pvt.	D, E
WOODFORD, J. B.	Pvt.	D, E
WOODFORD, W. C.	Pvt.	D, E
WOODHAM, A. JEHU	Pvt.	H, E
WORD, W. H.	1 Lt., Cpl.	H
WREN, G. R.	Pvt.	B, E
WREN, W. T.	Pvt.	B, E
WRIGHT, ELIAS	Pvt.	H
WRIGHT, JAMES M.	Cpl.	H, E

WRIGHT, JAMES S.	Pvt.	D, E
WRIGHT, M. F.	Sgt.	B, E
WRIGHT, R. G.	Capt., Maj.	B, F&S, E
WRILEY, T.	Pvt.	C
WROTEN, THOMAS L.	Pvt.	B
WYATT, I.	Pvt.	-
YARBOROUGH, J. N.	Pvt.	F, E
YARBROUGH, G. W.	Pvt.	F
YARBROUGH, J. W.	-	E
YELVERTON, WILLIAM G.	Capt.	K
YOCUM, GEORGE W.	Pvt.	A
YOUNG, ANDERSON H.	Pvt.	K
YOUNG, JOHN L.	Pvt.	A, E
YOUNG, S. W.	2 Lt.	K, E
YOUNG, WILLIAM W.	Pvt.	C, E
ZILLS, JAMES P.	Pvt.	K, E
ZILLS, W. P.	Pvt.	K, E
ZIMMERMAN, JOHN	Pvt.	I, E

Appendix II

27th Alabama Infantry Regiment

Organization: Organized by the increase of Foster's Infantry Battalion to a regiment at Fort Heiman on December 28, 1861. Surrendered at Fort Donelson on February 16, 1862. Survivors attached to the 33rd Mississippi Infantry regiment. Exchanged at Vicksburg, Mississippi on September 4, 1862. Reorganized at Jackson, Mississippi in October 1862. Field consolidation with the 35th and 49th Infantry Regiments from July 1864 to April 9, 1865.

First Commander: Adolphus A. Hughes (Colonel)

The regiment was organized in December 1861, at Fort Heiman, Tennessee. Its companies were recruited in Franklin, Lauderdale, Lawrence, Mobile, Madison, and Morgan counties. The unit was sent to Fort Henry, then Fort Donelson where it was captured on February 16, 1862. However, a number of men were sick in the hospital and escaped the surrender. These men were organized into two companies, joined a Mississippi regiment, and at the Battle of Perryville lost 8 killed and 25 wounded. The main body of the regiment was exchanged, reunited with the other two companies at Port Hudson, and assigned to Beall's and Buford's Brigade, Department of Mississippi and East Louisiana. The 27th was engaged at Champion's Hill and Big Black River Bridge, served in the trenches at Jackson, and later moved with the army across the Pearl River. During the spring of 1864, it joined the Army of Tennessee and, attached to General Scott's and Shelley's Brigade, participated in many conflicts from Resaca to Bentonville. Only a remnant surrendered on April 26, 1865.

Battles: Fort Henry (February 6, 1862)
Fort Donelson (February 12–16, 1862)

123

Vicksburg Campaign (May–July 1863)
Champion Hill (May 16, 1863)
Jackson Siege (July 1863)
Meridian Campaign (February–March 1864)
Morton (February 8, 1864)
Chunky Mountain (February 12, 1864)
Moulton (March 21, 1864)
near Florence, Alabama (April 12, 1864)
Atlanta Campaign (May–September 1864)
Resaca (May 14–15, 1864)
New Hope Church (May 25–June 4, 1864)
Kennesaw Mountain (June 27, 1864)
Peach Tree Creek (July 20, 1864)
Ezra Church (July 28, 1864)
Atlanta Siege (July–September 1864)
Jonesboro (August 21–September 1, 1864)
Ackworth (October 4, 1864)
Franklin (November 30, 1864)
Nashville (December 15–16, 1864)
Carolinas Campaign (February–April 1865)
Kinston (March 7–10, 1865)
Bentonville (March 19–21, 1865)

THE CIVIL WAR AS SEEN BY CAPTAIN ISAAC JASPER ROGERS, COMPANY B, 27TH ALABAMA VOLUNTEER INFANTRY REGIMENT

By Charles E. Wilson

Isaac Jasper Rogers was born June 2, 1835, in Jefferson County, Alabama.* He was born approximately six miles west of Elyton, not far from the Elyton-Jonesboro road called Stoney Lonesome. His boyhood was spent roving the woods on Red and Sand (now called Rock or West Red) Mountains. In this prosperous region, he attended schools and the protracted meetings held by the circuit riding preachers. At one of the meetings at Salem Springs Church, a few miles below Bessemer today, he joined the Missionary Baptist Church. These meetings made a great impression on his mind and were partly the reason for his life-long religious fervor. The schools, which met at short intervals, were held near the present day town of Powderly, now in the Birmingham City limits, and near Jonesboro (Bessemer). The schooling he received there was later used to good advantage.

In 1850, his parents, John B. and Margaret Rogers, decided to move to Franklin County. Selling the homestead, they moved by wagon to Pleasant Site, Alabama. Here young Rogers continued his studies, attending the country schools

* For the lineage of Isaac Jasper Rogers, see Harry V. Bernard, "John William Rogers" Annals of Northwest Alabama (Tuscaloosa, 1959), II, 76–86.

which met at short intervals. He spent a good deal of time studying at home, and when he had mastered the "Old Blueback Spelling Book", he began to look around for employment. Friends and neighbors considered him competent to teach, so he took the examination for the position and passed. He modestly reported that he "seemed to give satisfaction" but records indicate that he was one of the best teachers of that area, teaching both at the Pleasant Site and Rock Creek schools.

By the spring of 1861, I. J. Rogers had accumulated a small amount of money, and still lived with his parents. He had long wanted to go west and seek his fortune like so many others had done in the past ten years. So, he set out "with heavy heart" and landed in Arkansas in March of 1861. Arkansas was so impressive to him that he decided to make it his future home. He again found his school training valuable for he taught a short school there. He also worked at other things and took one trip into the Indian nation to Fort Smith. Meanwhile, the War Between the States had broken out and was growing worse day by day. The excitement and confusion that raged made everyone anxious to do his part in the forthcoming struggle. I. J. Rogers was determined to return home and join the Confederate Army with his friends. He arrived in Pleasant Site in September 1861 and was intending to volunteer at once. Typhoid fever struck him, however, and it was not until Christmas that he was able to get out of the house.

When the call went out from General Polk, in the Fall of 1861, for volunteers to "defend their hearths", the Federals were already threatening Columbus, Kentucky. General Polk called for North Alabamians to defend their river forts, alerting them that the fall of the forts on the Tennessee would mean the loss of the Tennessee Valley to the enemy. Adolphus A. Hughes, a member of the legislature, from Franklin County, received permission to organize a number of companies to form the 27th Alabama Volunteer Infantry Regiment. Hughes' energy and the help of another representative, T. J. Foster of Lawrence County, quickly filled the companies with good men from Franklin, Lawrence, Morgan, Madison, and Lauderdale Counties.

A. A. Hughes was elected Colonel, shortly after the regiment was organized, replacing T. J. Foster under whose name the regiment was organized. Indeed, the regiment was known as "Foster's Regiment" for some time. James Jackson was elected Lieutenant Colonel, and Dr. Edward McAlexander, from Lauderdale County, was made Major. Company commanders were as follows:

Company A., Capt. J. E. Moore (Franklin); Company B., Capt. R. G. Wright (Franklin); Company C., Capt. Thompson (Lauderdale); Company D., Capt. H. B. Irwin (Lawrence); Company E., Capt. T. A. Jones (Lauderdale); Company F., Capt. Roberts (Madison); Company G., Capt. Thomas McCulloch (Franklin); Company H., Capt. Humphrey (Morgan); Company I., Capt. Henry McGhee (Lawrence); Company K., Capt. Ray (Lauderdale).

Company B the "Confederate Sentinels" was being organized at Pleasant Site just as I. J. Rogers was getting over his attack of fever, so he joined as a private in that company. He was promptly elected First Sergeant of the company, with only one vote against him. The men were mustered-in at Florence, Alabama, on the 19th day of December, 1861. The regiment remained at Florence until the 1st of January, 1862, when it proceeded down the Tennessee River to Fort Henry by steamship. The 27th was camped on the South bank of the river, where some companies from North Alabama were already in camp. When all the companies had arrived, the men elected officers. The weather was unpleasant and the campsite, being in a low area, caused a great deal of sickness.

The troops were very willing but were unaccustomed to life of a soldier, so they later were amused by their first camp life. They had brought tremendous quantities of clothing, tents, and as one soldier described it, they carried everything but a bed... and for that they carried a ticking which they filled with straw. Rations soon became more scarce, however, and some of them began to feel that the life of a soldier wasn't as romantic as it had been pictured. As the ground became muddy and measles broke out, some of the men became sick and died. Although they complained of their bad luck and troubles, they were really in very pleasant circumstances compared to that which was to come shortly.

Their training was good, and many nights they were awakened by the roll of the drum and the bugle, signifying the call to line of battle. Early on the night of February 4th, a loud call came, but again it proved to be false. Not long after, the officers came around and told everyone to get up and leave everything except the weapons. Most of the men were armed with shotguns and had buckshot for ammunition. The men then left their comfortable tents, moved across the river and marched out to the breastworks. Some of them camped in a small woods. That day was one of waiting in the cold, for all the blankets and tents had been left on the other side of the river. It began to rain toward night and the entire regiment was without shelter. The rain continued during the entire night of the 5th. When the 6th came, all were cold and hungry. At one o'clock gunboats began firing on the fort and demolished most of the Confederate guns. General Tilghman, Commander of the Fort, surrendered unconditionally.

Colonel Heiman, meanwhile, was in charge of the 27th. He was from the 10th Tennessee Regiment and he directed the retreat toward Fort Donelson. It was a circuitous march, across heavy streams and, as a result, most of the artillery and a good many prisoners were lost. The march lasted all night, through trees and woods and over very difficult terrain. After twenty miles, the regiment attempted to reform, and the men discovered that everything had been thrown away to make the speedy retreat...overcoats, baggage and all, except weapons. On the next day the regiments arrived at Fort Donelson, without beds or blankets. The weather was extremely cold and the suffering was great. Many cases of frostbite and frozen hands and feet were reported from the cold and the dampness the troops had been through. On the 12th General Pillow ordered them into line of battle at Fort Donelson and the 27th Regiment marched out to the expected point of attack.

Forrest's cavalry rode out and engaged the advance, but no other firing occurred during that day. At night on the 12th, the work began on throwing up fortifications and when daylight arrived, a very admirable defense had been completed.

On the 13th cannonading began with little damage to either side. The Federal forces attacked the left wing but were driven back. Again at 12 o'clock another sortie was made against the Alabamians, but again the Yankees retreated with heavy loss, while Confederate losses were very slight.

That night the gunboats made an attack on the fort, but were driven back with heavy damage to their boats, and the Confederate losses were one killed and two or three wounded. It began to sleet shortly afterward and, then, a heavy snow storm covered the ground to the depth of several inches. Because of the closeness to the enemy, no fires were permitted; therefore, the suffering was very great that night.

When the dawn of the 14th came, firing began again and continued throughout the day with great damage to the enemy, but with little damage to the Confederates. The breastworks protected the Confederate position very well. It was learned, however, that the Federals were massing reinforcements. Because it was felt that the 27th Regiment's position would be overpowered, it was determined that the men should attack the extreme right of the Federal lines and make a way out at daybreak. Everything was made ready and at daylight the firing began. So successful was the attack, that the enemy was driven back two miles. The officers then held a parley and decided they could hold the position; therefore, the fort was not evacuated while the way was opened. Late that evening, the Confederates left their breastworks and attacked the enemy in their own positions. This was the first real fight the Alabamians had faced, and they found the Federals waiting for them. The Federal forces soon retreated leaving knapsacks and blankets behind. Again the Confederate loss was slight, while the Federal loss was heavy. Later that evening, the Federals attacked and got into the breastworks, but were repelled. In the words of Sergeant I. J. Rogers, "...we whipped [sic] them on every part of the ground all day Saturday." By that time, however, the Confederates were nearly worn out from fighting and from having been on the line of battle four days and nights. It began raining, sleeting and snowing, the clothes freezing on the men. That night the enemy reinforced themselves heavily. Because the enemy constantly poured fresh men against them, the Confederate Generals felt they should not risk another engagement, so, they decided to surrender. It was a great surprise to the men, however, on the morning of the 16th, to see a white flag hoisted and to hear the officers tell them that they were prisoners of war.* That Sunday morning the enemy marched in and took over government

* *Because the men were surprised at the action of the surrendering officers, later a great deal was said about the surrender of Fort Donelson. Many claimed that it was not necessary to surrender. However, later testimony verified the fact that overwhelming forces were against them at that time, and that the mistake in strategy was made in remaining in the fort. Yorktown is an example of such military strategy in which the commanders allowed troops to get bottled up without escape. The reinforcements which Johnston had sent were not utilized properly, too, and the surrender is not generally considered the result of poor tactics and coordination on the part of the Southern generals at the scene.*

stores and the troops made ready to march off to they knew not where. They expected parole, but it was not granted.

On the 17th, the Confederate prisoners of war were carried down the Cumberland River on the Steamer "White Cloud"—the first leg of their journey to Camp Douglas, Illinois. The cold was extreme, and there was no way of cooking the meager rations which were given the prisoners. The voyage lasted about a week and the crowded conditions of 1000 men on the steamer made the voyage a terrible one. At St. Louis, the prisoners were put on the railroad for Chicago. Sixty men were crowded into a car.

Two nights and one day were required to make the trip from St. Louis to Chicago. All that time the men were without fire, the ground was covered with snow, and the weather was freezing cold. When the enlisted men reached Chicago, they were marched through town and to Camp Douglas, where they were given quarters.

The company officers were sent to Johnson's Island, Ohio; the field officers to Fort Warren, Massachusetts.

Camp Douglas contained about 100 acres and was walled in by a plank fence. The houses inside had stoves and would have been fairly comfortable if there had been sufficient room, but the crowded conditions made them very disagreeable. Although there was plenty to eat at first, the water did not agree with the prisoners and, as a result, many died. Others died from exposure, for there were no blankets and the thin clothing of the prisoners was not adequate to protect them from the freezing weather. The prisoners never saw the ground because of snow between the 13th of February and the 1st of April when the snow finally cleared. After the thaw came, the low position of the camp on Lake Michigan caused the ground to be very muddy, making the camp's condition even more uncomfortable. About eighty thousand troops were quartered at Camp Douglas; therefore, the constant tramping kept the mud worked up "like a hog pen."

Many prisoners attempted escape; some made it, others were brought back and still others were shot in the attempt.

Conversation among the prisoners was, in general, about getting out and being exchanged, going home, or telling of the hardships already past and speculating on the future. Most of the time was spent in sitting around the stoves and talking, the weather being so cold that nothing else was practicable. There was preaching nearly every day when the weather was good. Sometimes this was done by Southerners, and other times Northern preachers would come in and do the preaching.

The snow was about knee deep on the 21st of April, and it was about the 23rd that I. J. Rogers became ill for several days. Luckily, the weather turned out pleasant on the 25th and the first good weather since the capture made him recuperate rapidly.

The month of May was ushered in by cold rain and sleet, but by the middle of the month the weather was warmer and the trees began to bud. When spring finally did arrive, the prisoners were more discontented than ever. Toward the end of May, Sergeant Rogers became afflicted with rheumatism and sore eyes at the same time.

In August, about one hundred prisoners escaped but about a dozen of them were recaptured and punished by being made to walk around camp with a sign on their backs reading, "This Escaped Prisoner Recaptured."

I. J. Rogers received news from home for the first time on the 7th of August. He was saddened to find that his younger brother, Wesley, had been killed at the Battle of Shiloh in April. During the Spring and Summer the prisoners played ball, marbles, and other games for amusement. Reading was a favorite pastime, and there were fortunately a large supply of books available. Sergeant Rogers read his Testament through twice during his imprisonment.

Around the first of September there was news that prisoners were to be exchanged, and accordingly the 27th was released on the 4th of September.*

The way back down the river was exciting after having been confined for so many months, and the troops were met by many Southern women who waved, and gave them food whenever possible. Ladies in Memphis met the boat and gave the soldiers food and other items such as soap, fruit and clothing. On the 16th of September the boat arrived opposite Vicksburg, Mississippi, and the troops were released on the following day. There they crossed the river to find dinner cooked and waiting for them. This was a day of great rejoicing for the prisoners who had returned, However, it was tempered with sadness for, of the number captured, almost one-third had died. Two hundred and eighty were captured, and of that number, eighty-two had been left on what was then enemy soil.

On the 18th the group left Vicksburg for Jackson with their officers, who having been already exchanged were waiting for the men when they arrived in Vicksburg. They arrived in Jackson, marched out to the old Fair Grounds, camped there three or four days, and then moved about four miles out of town. While in Jackson, the Regiment was reorganized and the same officers were reelected.

On the 24th of September, I. J. Rogers was elected a 1st Lieutenant in the company. The regiment was thrown into two companies and consolidated with the 1st Mississippi and the 9th Tennessee regiments. Colonel Simington of the 1st Mississippi commanded the unit. After drawing clothing, blankets, and guns,

---

*At the time of the capture of the 27th, so many men were in hospitals and other places because of epidemics of diseases of different kinds, that, along with those not captured, enough men for two companies were soon ready for combat. These companies were assigned to the 33rd Mississippi under Col. A. B. Hardcastle. Company officers were Captain Wright, with Lt. R. T. Harris., Lt. F. Le B. Goodwin and Lt. H. Rogers; Capt. William Wood, Lieutenant Cunningham, Lieutenant Chandler and Lieutenant Andrews. Capt. T. A. Jones, who escaped from Donelson, was made major of 33rd. The two companies were designated I and K of the 33rd Mississippi. They went from Corinth to Tupelo, from Chattanooga, through Bragg's campaign in Kentucky and back to Shelbyville, Tenn. These companies lost heavily at Perryville on October 8. Captain Wood was killed.

The 33rd was in Brig. Gen. S. A. M. Wood's brigade, General Buckner's division. When the 27th was exchanged, the men remaining in the 33rd applied to be returned to their original regiment and it was granted.

the regiment moved to Holly Springs. Here all the surplus officers were sent to North Alabama to recruit. Lt. Rogers, however, remained in the regiment. After a few days, the unit was ordered to Port Hudson, Louisiana. At this point the members of the 27th who had been in the Army of Tennessee and Kentucky, under Bragg, rejoined their group (see footnote 5).

Shortly after the arrival at Port Hudson, Colonel A. A. Hughes the Regimental Commander died of disease, and Lt. Colonel James Jackson was promoted to Colonel. McAlexander was made Lt. Col., Capt. Wright of Company B was made Major. With this shifting, Lt. Watson was made Captain and commander of Company B, and Lt. F. Le B. Goodwin was made commander of Company A.

Port Hudson was about twenty-five miles north of Baton Rouge. The conditions were not favorable for the troops stationed there. During their month stay, many men had dysentery and one man died of small pox; but, the severe isolation of the cases kept this disease from spreading. Rations consisted of cornbread, blue beef, sugar and rice. The bread was not good, for the meal was coarse and unsifted. The sugar was of a syrupy brown variety and the rice was poor quality. Finally, when some pork was received the morale was heightened.

On the 1st of March the Federal forces sent a fleet of boats against Port Hudson, making a night attack on the water batteries. They were driven back, badly damaged, and the expected land attack never materialized because of the damage sustained on the river craft. The Confederate units were under heavy firing which commenced at 11 o'clock, but soon was quiet again.

About the 1st of April, when everything had been quiet for a good length of time, all troops which could be spared were ordered to Tullahoma, Tennessee. A new brigade composed of the troops remaining at Port Hudson was formed, with General Buford of Kentucky in charge. The new unit consisted of the 27th, 35th, and 55th Alabama regiments; the 3rd, 7th and 8th Kentucky regiments and the 9th Arkansas.

Accordingly, on the 6th of April, the 27th left Port Hudson and marched sixty miles to board the New Orleans and Jackson Railroad for Jackson, where they arrived on the night of the 14th of April. Upon arrival, Lt. Rogers applied for a leave to visit home for he had not had leave since his enlistment. This being granted he travelled by train to Meridian, then to Oklaona, and then seventy miles by foot to his home. He arrived on the 19th, after sixteen months away from home. After his visit to Franklin County, Alabama, he had planned to meet the brigade at Stevenson, Alabama, thinking the unit would be going to Tennessee. However, after a week at home, he left for Decatur, then to Huntsville where he learned that his Regiment had been ordered back to Mississippi. The 27th had got only as far as Montgomery—some as far as Selma—before they returned to Mississippi. When Lt. Rogers arrived back at Jackson, Mississippi, he had travelled by the way of Chattanooga, Atlanta, Montgomery, Selma, Meridian and then to Jackson. Transportation difficulty necessitated this circuitous trip. Therefore, by the time he rejoined the 27th at Jackson, the unit was just coming out of the battle of Baker's Creek. Buford's Brigade had been put in Loring's Division upon its return to Jackson.*

When the city of Vicksburg was surrendered, the entire Federal force was then turned on the little army of Johnston. Therefore, the Confederate force was moved back to Jackson to make a stand. Several attempts were made to penetrate the fortifications they set-up there, but all were unsuccessful. During the stand of Jackson, the 27th was unfortunate to get into a bad position before it could prepare defenses. Featherstone's regiment was placed directly before the main force and the 27th was at right angles to it on the right flank. Therefore, every Federal shell or bullet that penetrated the area of the 27th enfiladed through the whole regiment. Finally, the men were able to dig trenches and cross-trench the area for their protection.

While the digging was going on General Johnston came riding up and asked why there were so many ditches. Someone answered, "You'll see when a shell comes along." About that time a shell came through and Johnston laughed and said, "The explanation is satisfactory." One of the guns got the range of the 27th and kept lobbing shells into the area. Each company kept a man on lookout, and in the daytime when he'd see a puff of smoke or at night a flash, he'd yell, "watch out." This was the signal for everyone to jump into a trench. As a result of this strategy no one was killed or wounded as a result of the shelling.

The siege of Jackson never amounted to a real battle, but was only skirmishing. On the 14th a truce was declared for the purpose of burying the dead. A peace spread over the whole area for the first time in a number of days. Many of the soldiers strolled out and talked to Union troops. At four o'clock, however, the drums announced the truce was over and everyone hastened back to the ditches.

On the 16th, it was discovered that the Federals were attempting to pass behind the Confederate lines, the division pulled out and left only pickets firing.

The unit then moved on the Southern Railway to Meridian, Mississippi. It was here that Captain Watson, Commander of Company B, deserted on July 17th leaving Company B without a commander. They then moved on to Morton's Station and Forest Station but the Federals did not pursue.

At this time troops were badly needed in Tennessee, so Walker's and Breckenridge's divisions were sent as reinforcements. Loring's Division remained in Mississippi, and as Grant moved back to Vicksburg, the division moved back to Canton for the winter. Lt. Rogers was promoted to Captain and Company Commander in place of Watson.

When the men first built their winter quarters near Canton, they made them of Johnson grass and other materials. While they were out on patrol duty, the farmers used the soldiers' houses for winter feed. There were some angry

---

* *The Battle of Baker's Creek occurred on May 16, 1863. The 27th was heavily engaged and retreated. In the retreat from the field, Capt. W. A. Isbell of Co. G. (Franklin County, Ala.) was struck by a random shot. He died the next day. Lt. S. S. Anderson was promoted to his place.*

soldiers for awhile, but they then decided to build their quarters out of more substantial materials.

While encamped near Canton, a revival was begun by Chaplain Coffee, assisted by Dr. Burns and Lt. Davis of the 12th Louisiana Regiment. The men gathered pine knots and illuminated the grounds at night and the revival was well attended. A Christian Association was formed and the membership grew very large through the revival.

One morning Colonel Jackson walked through the 27th's camp and facetiously remarked that he was glad the 27th didn't have any corn cobs and shuck lying around. General Buford was planning to inspect that morning. The men got busy and picked up an entire wagon load of shucks and corn cobs, and buried them in a pine thicket. They got brush brooms and swept and straightened up the area.

When General Buford rode through he said, "Jackson, this beats the devil." "What's the matter, General?" "The 27th Alabama is the only regiment in the Confederacy that eats corn, cobs and shucks without leaving any sign." He finally rode off and visited the 9th Arkansas. There he found plenty of cobs and shucks. He marched them all afternoon until they were dead tired.

On the 23rd of December, Captain Rogers was furloughed home for twenty-five days. He rejoined the company on the 20th of January at Canton, Mississippi. About the 1st of February, a heavy force was sent from Vicksburg under General Sherman. The Confederate force consisted of French's and Loring's divisions with Jackson's cavalry. These units fell back toward Meridian in a well conducted retreat under General Polk, General Johnston having been sent to take command of the Army of Tennessee in December. The retreat continued to Demopolis, Alabama. Reinforcements from Tennessee arrived, and the Federal cavalry received a bad whipping from General Forrest's cavalry.

The Federals withdrew to Vicksburg in haste and the 27th Regiment was sent to Mount Hope, Alabama on a recruiting expedition. However, the occupation of the Tennessee Valley by Federals kept the 27th from recruiting successfully. The most exciting event of the entire trip was a guerilla-type raid across the Tennessee on the 13th of April. A Yankee Captain, two lieutenants and about forty men were captured. Also about one hundred head of horses and mules, two or three hundred beef cattle, bacon, guns, and other equipment. Only one man was lost.

Back at Mount Hope, the unit received orders to rejoin the Army they had left in Mississippi. They marched about 160 miles to Montevallo. Here they rejoined their Alabama division and took the train to Blue Mountain near Anniston, Alabama, marched through Rome, Georgia, to Kinston where they took the Chattanooga Railway to Resacca. There, on the 11th of May, the troops met General Johnston's army retreating from Dalton.

After the 16th the Confederate forces pulled back toward Atlanta. The force made many such stands and held the Federal forces in check as long as possible, sometimes weeks at a time, before pulling back to make another stand.

Skirmishing continued day and night for many weeks, killing and wounding many men; the Federals suffering more casualties than the Confederates. Because the Federals outnumbered the troops of the South, the retreating and holding movement continued until the Chattahoochee River was crossed, There the men enjoyed several days of rest. Johnston had managed the army with great skill and every man was acquainted with the tactics and the plan that they were following. General Johnston had thwarted the enemy in every battle. Thus, it was surprising to the men when Johnston was relieved of command of the Army and General Hood was placed in command. Captain Rogers stated, "We hated very much to part with old Joe as all familirly [*sic*] called him but we had to give him up and trust to an inexperienced officer."

When the Federal forces began to cross the river on the extreme right wing, on the 20th of July, 1864, Hood ordered his forces out to meet them. They were given instructions to let nothing stop them and went forward with real determination. The Federals had built strong breastworks. At these breastworks the charge was brought to a standstill and the fighting became desperate. Again the orders were sent to take the works, the 27th being in the foremost of the fighting. Some Federal troops had occupied a house near the line and were pouring a galling fire down on the Confederate front line troops. Colonel Jackson took some men with him and charged and captured the house. He received a bullet in his arm that necessitated the amputation of the arm. John E. Abernathy captured the colors of a New Jersey regiment. Several pieces of artillery were also captured but had to be abandoned because the right flank of the brigade had to advance through an open field and could not come up. This made a failure of the whole charge, and the only alternative was to retreat and leave the wounded and dead in the hands of the Federals. The two brigades of the division which were engaged lost about half their men each. Adam's brigade was not engaged.

In a few days the units fell back to Atlanta and began preparing defensive positions. Hardy's Corps passed through Atlanta and fell on the extreme left wing of the Federals, driving them two miles back, killing and capturing a great many men and capturing about twenty pieces of artillery. The Federals then gave up their right flanking movement, concentrating on the left. Therefore, Hood determined to attack again and in the battle the Confederate forces were repulsed. Generals Stewart and Loring were wounded and many officers and men were lost. The Confederates fell back to their former positions and strengthened themselves, while the Federals moved up to close range and threw up fortifications of their own. They flanked batteries on every hill and cannonading and skirmishing continued until about the last of August without a general engagement. Picket and line duty was very hard on the troops with the hot August sun beating down upon them. Captain Rogers had four holes shot through his clothing and one through his cap during this picketing duty.

The 27th soon became so small that General Scott ordered it consolidated with the 35th and 49th Alabama Regiments. That left Captain Rogers without a command, so he was ordered to take command of the 56th Alabama Dismounted

Cavalry. This was in Sears' Brigade, French's Division. He remained with this Division during the remainder of the siege of Atlanta.

On the 14th of September Captain Rogers was ordered to North Alabama on another recruiting mission. He reached home on the 20th and remained a month, but his efforts to recruit men to the banners of the Confederacy were in vain. He rejoined the army in Tuscumbia, Alabama, and was in Hood's campaign in Nashville, Tennessee. Hood moved toward Franklin, Tennessee, and then stopped his march to Nashville before he reached the city, waiting for reinforcements. So close did the Federal troops pass the waiting Confederates that they could hear them moving. By the time Hood attacked in Franklin the Union forces were already dug in. That battle was on November 20, 1864. This battle has been described as a valorous but costly failure for the South. Schofield, the Union general lost 2000 men; Hood lost over 6000.

The Union forces then were put under siege in Nashville and remained so until December 15th. The lack of activity on the part of Thomas caused his superiors to become impatient with him. They sent Logan to supersede him. Thomas, however, to retain command attacked just before Logan's assumption of command and pushed Hood into the two-day battle of Nashville. This battle destroyed the remaining forces of the fine army Johnston had built in the Atlanta campaign. At the close of that battle, of the 1000 who left Alabama in 1861 as members of the proud 27th Regiment, only 17 were left—one-half of these being officers. The 27th, 35th and 49th had neither Colonel, nor Lt. Colonel, nor Major, according to Captain Rogers. Since he was the only Captain left of the ten, the command of the regiment was his responsibility. He, therefore, made application for the men to be furloughed home.

The men reassembled at Tupelo, Mississippi, and were sent immediately to Kinston, North Carolina. They arrived there on the 9th of March, 1865. They were placed on the firing line. Captain Rogers led 60 men to take the place of men who had been on it for long periods of time.

On the night of March 9, soon after the 27th arrived in North Carolina, it began to rain, so Captain Rogers sat under a tree and put a blanket over his head to sleep. He was aroused at daybreak by pickets firing. He got up and went into the skirmish, and was shot in the foot. He was then carried to a hospital at Chesterfield, South Carolina. Here he remained until he was paroled, on May 6, 1865, along with the others in the Army of Tennessee.

Captain Rogers returned home and remained at home until his mother's death in 1872. During that time he worked on the railroad near Burnville, Mississippi, getting wood in order to help buy corn and supplies to help his father and brother, Jake, make a crop.

A friend promised to send Captain Rogers through a course of study of medicine. He studied closely for a while, and one year was spent in it. Then Dr. A. M. Chate said Rogers was fully prepared to take the course of medical lectures. The benefactor then informed Captain Rogers that he could not send him, and a year was lost.

Again he decided to go west because of the bad luck in getting work. His parents encouraged him to stay with them, so he did. In 1872 his mother died, and shortly afterward, his father. Captain Rogers was now 36 and penniless.

In 1870, he was elected County Superintendent of Education of Franklin County, Alabama. He served six years and then resigned and bought a little farm near Pleasant Site. Shortly afterward he married Rebecca J. Weatherford of Frankfort, Alabama. In the fall of 1881 they sold the farm and moved to Burleson, Alabama, and went into the mercantile business. His wife died in 1906. He died in 1908, the father of eleven children.

Appendix IV

The magazine *Confederate Veteran* was printed from 1893 to 1932. During this 39-year history several mentions were made of the 27th Alabama Infantry. These editors have put together several of the more interesting of these articles to allow the reader more insight into the men that served in this regiment. These articles should provide both a genealogy and historic interest to the reader.

Dr. J. P. Cannon, McKenzie, Tenn.: "If the Confederate officer who was arrested on the train between Chattanooga and Atlanta about the 1st of December, 1862, is living, I would be glad for him to write to me. I can not recall his name, but he was a major on some general's staff (I think Gen. Buckner's), and attempted to get me through on his passport. Both of us were arrested and brought back to Chattanooga."

W. A. Benham.
Comrade W. A. Benham died at his home, in Wills Point, Tex., February 24, 1915. He was born in Florence, Ala., February 13, 1846, and there reared and educated. He joined the Confederate army in January, 1862, as a member of Company E, 27th Alabama Infantry, commanded by Col. James Jackson. He was captured at Fort Donelson in February, 1862, and taken to Camp Douglas, Chicago. He was afterwards exchanged at Vicksburg, Miss. He reenlisted and was again taken prisoner and sent to Rock Island Prison. He was married to Miss Mattie Marks, of Lauderdale County, Ala., in 1867. They moved to Texas in 1869. He was a Mason for thirty-five years and a consistent member of the Methodist Episcopal Church, South. He had been a member of the Wills Point Camp, No. 302, U. C. V., since its organization. His cheerful disposition made him a welcome visitor anywhere.

W. T. Grice

W. T. Grice, of Quitman, Wood County, Tex., wants to hear from any of his old comrades who can testify to his service as a Confederate soldier. He belonged to Company C, 27th Alabama Infantry. Just after the war he removed to Texas from his old home in Alabama, and he has not been able to get in touch with any of his war comrades. He is trying to get a pension.

SIX BROTHERS CONFEDERATE SURVIVORS

A comrade sends a photograph of six brothers, all of who served in the Confederate army, and who are yet living and in fair health, with notes by H. A. Killen, of Green Hill, Ala.

Dunkin, Dan, and I volunteered October 6, 1861, in Company E, Twenty-Seventh Alabama Regiment. Our services began at Fort Henry. We were next at Corinth, and after that went through the campaign in Kentucky under Gen. Bragg. We were afterwards at Port Hudson. We were there the night of that terrific bombardment in which the "Mississippi", a noted Federal gunboat, was destroyed by our hotshot battery on the river bank. We were in the battle of Baker's Creek, Miss., and escaped capture by passing out at night through a swamp. We were also in the siege of Jackson, Miss., after which we were sent to North Alabama to recruit. While in that service we crossed the Tennessee River and captured a company of the Ninth Ohio Regiment. Going next to Georgia, we joined the Army of Tennessee at Resaca. We were in the beginning of that battle, and afterwards participated in many of the engagements of that "hundred days fighting". We next went to Nashville in Hood's army. On the retreat my two brothers were left on picket duty at Duck River. The pontoon was taken up, and "Dunk" lay under the bluff three days, and the only food he had was an ear of corn. He finally escaped by wading a creek at night. I was the only member of my company in the battle of Bentonville, and there were but seven of the regiment in the surrender there. Tom and Jackson were in Forrest's Cavalry; I do not know the regiment. They were in several engagements. Robert was just old enough to enlist in the latter part of the war, but was not in any of the battles. I was promoted from a private to lieutenant, and commanded the company much of the time, as my captain was on detached service. None of the six were wounded or in hospital. Tom was captured and imprisoned at Rock Island.

FROM THE WESTERN BORDER OF TEXAS

Comrades in the far West are diligent in the sacred duties incumbent upon them. A new camp has been organized in far West Texas with a membership extending over six of those large counties. Comrade H. O'Neal, of Alpine, has been elected Commander. He writes:

I take pleasure in writing to what a few old veterans in this county are doing. We like the *Veteran* very much, and would not do without it. We have organized a camp on the Texas frontier, and our population is scattered. Some of us will go to Nashville to the reunion.

I was only thirteen years old when I enlisted in Company A, Fortieth Alabama Regiment, at Demopolis. My first battle was at Chickasaw Bayou, near Vicksburg, Miss., and, by accident, I was not captured at the surrender of Vicksburg. I was also at Lookout Mountain and Missionary Ridge, and at both places I eluded capture by the "blue boys". I was in the Georgia campaign from Dalton to Atlanta, and never missed a battle. In the battle of New Hope Church the Twenty-seventh Alabama Regiment was cut to pieces; in fact, nearly all killed. I remember that one shell killed twenty-one men, struck the breastworks and scattered the rails. I lost some of my best friends there, among them Pole Dearman and Bob McGowan.

The 22d, 23d, and 28th of July were hard battles for us, and we lost a great many good men. I would like to know what became of one of my friends, Hyram Fincher, who was wounded on the 28th. The enemy drove us back, and afterwards I went to look for him, but could not find him.

Selected Documents
of the
27th Alabama Infantry

Lieutenant Colonel Alexander's pay voucher dated October 31, 1863.

Invoice of Arms & Ordn Stores
Turned in to J W Boring
act ordn offr March 3d 1864

1	✓	Rifle cal 58
2	✓	Muskets cal 69
1	✓	Bay for Sam
13	✓	Cartg Box
14	✓	Cap Pouches
30	✓	Cart Box Belts
13	✓	Waist Belts
4	✓	Bay Scabbards
4380	✓	cartgs cal 58
2225	✓	cartgs cal 54
1820	✓	B & B cal 69
600	✓	Gun Caps
6	✓	Canteens
12	✓	Packing Boxs

James Jackson
Col 25" alus Bvt

Invoice of arms and ammunition for March 3, 1864, signed by Colonel Jackson.

Letter from Pvt. George M. Douglass asking for parole from Camp Douglas, Illinois, dated 1862.

Letter from Pvt. Thomas M. Irby asking for parole from Camp Douglas, Illinois dated July 7, 1862.

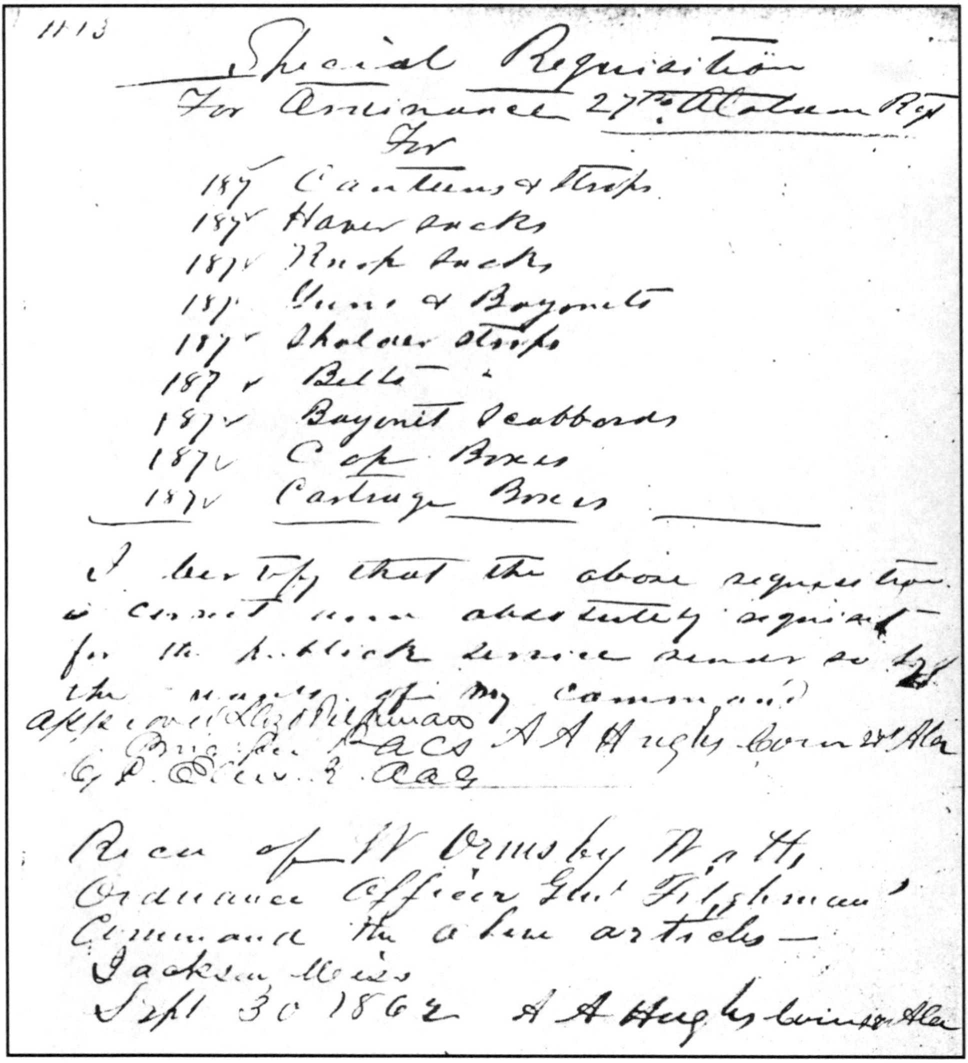

1113

Special Requisition
For Ordnance 27th Alabama Regt
For

187 Canteens & Straps
187 Haversacks
187 Knapsacks
187 Guns & Bayonets
187 Shoulder Straps
187 Belts
187 Bayonet Scabbards
187 Cap Boxes
187 Cartridge Boxes

I certify that the above requisition is correct and absolutely required for the public service rendered so by the usages of my command

Approved Lloyd Tilghman
Brig Genl Comdg
A A Hughes Comdg 27th Ala

Recd of W Ormsby Watts,
Ordnance Officer Genl Tilghman's
Command the above articles—
Jackson Miss
Sept 30 1862 A A Hughes Comdg 27th Ala

Special Requisition for Ordnance by Col. A. A. Hughes dated September 30, 1862.

Record of Death and Interment.

Name and number of person Interred	N. C. M. C. Curling ? ?
Number and locality of the grave	Cypress Grave Cemetery N° 2
Hospital number of the deceased	N° 472
Regiment, Rank and Company	Private Comp'y N 27 Alabama
Residence before Enlistment	
Conjugal Condition if married	
The residence of the widow	
Cause of Death	Diarrhoea Chronic
Age of the deceased	
Relatives and Remarks	
Date of the death and Burial	August 4, 1863

To

Brigadier Gen'. Thomas, Adj't Gen'. U. S. A.

Sir

It becomes my duty to Inform you that the person above described died at this Hospital as herein stated, and that it is desired his remains should be interred with the usual Military honors.

Respectfully.

Fr. C Bacon, Surgeon U. S. V.
In charge St Louis U. S. Gen'. Hosp.

Military Hosp'.
St Louis U. S. G. Hosp'

Record of Death and Interment Certificate dated August 4, 1863.

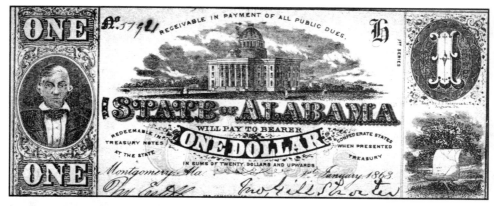

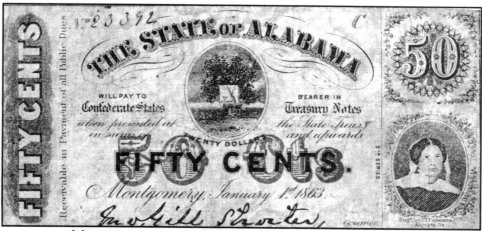

Alabama State money "redeemable" in Confederate treasury notes.

Noel Crowson's private collection

Photos of Members
of the
27th Alabama Infantry

The following pages contain the only known pictures of members of the 27th Alabama Infantry.

Six brothers Killen who were Confederates.
(1.) Andrew Jackson; (2.) Thomas Benton; (3.) Henry Alexander, 1st lieutenant, Company E; (4.) Dr. Duncan, corporal, Company E; (5.) Daniel McDougal, private, Company E; (6.) Robert Taylor

Confederate Veteran Magazine

Isaac Jasper Rogers, captain, Company B
Annals of Northwest Alabama

George W. Smith, private, Company A, E

U.S. Army Military History Institute

Thomas B. McCluskey, private, Company A, E

James T. Bolding, sergeant, Company B, E
U.S. Army Military History Institute

Bibliography

Barnard, Harry V. *Tattered Volunteers: The 27th Alabama Infantry Regiment C.S.A.* Hermitage Press: 1964.

Cannon, Jabez P. *Inside of Rebeldom: the Daily Life of a Private in the Confederate Army* (a series). Published in the Washington National Tribune: 1910.

Constable, George, editor. *The Civil War* (a series), Time Life Books. Various authors. Volumes 1–26.

Confederate Military History (a series). Various authors; edited by General Clement A. Evans. Tennessee State Library and Archives, Nashville, Tennessee. Blue and Gray Press: 1964.

Horne, Stanley F. Army of Tennessee. University of Oklahoma Press: 1952.

War of the Rebellion: Official Records of the Union and Confederate Armies. Published by the War Department, Washington D.C.: 1881–1900.

Microfilm

National Archives, Microfilm Military History Service Records, Group 109, rolls 83, 84, 93.

Index

153